NAPOLEON
IN CAPTIVITY

THE REPORTS OF COUNT BALMAIN RUSSIAN COMMISSIONER ON THE ISLAND OF ST HELENA 1816–1820

ALEKSANDR ANTONOVICH BALMAIN

Translated and Edited with
Introduction and Notes by
Julian Park
Revised with additional Notes by
Alan Sutton

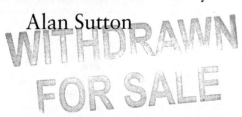

FONTHILL

Fonthill Media Limited
Fonthill Media LLC
www.fonthillmedia.com
office@fonthillmedia.com

First published in 1928.
This revised edition published in the United Kingdom
and the United States of America 2014.

British Library Cataloguing in Publication Data:
A catalogue record for this book is available from the British Library

Typeset in 10.5pt on 13pt Sabon LT Std
Printed and bound in England

CONTENTS

FOREWORD
TO THE 2014 EDITION

Professor Julian Park, (1888–1965), was Professor of European History at the University of Buffalo. He was the first dean of Arts and Sciences (1919–1954) and the University's first Historian (1959–1965) and he wrote the *History of the University of Buffalo* in 1917.

Park took an early interest in Count Balmain and this fascinating translation was first published in 1928.

This 2014 edition has been updated by Alan Sutton and the notes have been considerably expanded. The original edition had a few illustrations, but this revised edition includes a much wider and expanded selection of illustrations.

INTRODUCTION

1

Count Balmain's reports and letters, centring for four years around the circumstances of Napoleon's captivity, were written by one who never saw him. They are considered worthy of translation despite that fact, because they depict the extraordinary life on the 'rock' of St Helena (as the island of forty-seven square miles was generally termed) in probably as vivid and certainly as objective a manner as that of any of the innumerable company of contemporary writers.

By a treaty of 2 August 1815, the European powers, including France, were invited to send commissioners to the place to be chosen for Napoleon's detention, which the English had already decided was to be St Helena. This convention is referred to so often throughout these reports that it may well be given in full:

(1) Napoleon Buonaparte is considered by the Powers who have signed the Treaty of the 25th March last as their prisoner.

(2) His custody is especially intrusted to the British Government. The choice of the place, and of the measures which can best secure the object of the present stipulation, is reserved to his Britannic Majesty.

(3) The Imperial Courts of Austria and of Russia, and the Royal Court of Prussia, are to appoint Commissioners to proceed to and abide at the place which the Government of his Britannic Majesty shall have assigned for the residence of Napoleon Buonaparte, and who without being responsible for his custody will assure themselves of his presence.

(4) His Most Christian Majesty is to be invited, in the name of the four above-mentioned Courts, to send in the like manner a French Commissioner to the place of detention of Napoleon Buonaparte.

Prussia, probably for reasons of economy, sent no commissioner. The other three powers availed themselves of the invitation, and sent out representatives who found it easily possible to 'assure themselves of his presence' without ever laying eyes on the person of the prisoner of Europe.

Each of the three naturally sent to his government voluminous reports. The French and the Austrian were published respectively in 1894 and 1886; some of Count Balmain's reports were printed in the *Révue Bleue* in May and June, 1897, but a collected edition of them in English has never been published.

The choice of these three commissioners, or at least of two of them, is difficult to explain or to defend. None of them enjoyed anything like an outstanding reputation in his own country, and none of them would ever have been remembered by history were it not for the two, four, and five years which they spent on a tiny island in the South Atlantic. Of course this is true of many other people, for, with the possible exception of Bertrand, would the slightest shred of interest be otherwise attached to any member of the French retinue, or to the numerous English doctors who were thrown in contact with them, or the officers on duty at Longwood? Bertrand is the only one of importance who did not write one or more books, either at the time of the captivity or later; and that adds to our liking for him.

Naturally these contemporary or nearly contemporary accounts have all a highly personal thesis to maintain. Those of the French have value as source material for what actually happened at Longwood, but on most controversial subjects they are of course worthless. So also is Dr O'Meara's account (the famous *Voice from St Helena*), since his role was considerably more (or less) than that of a physician; and even the evidence left by the reputable doctors—from which class we must exclude Antommarchi—is somewhat affected by their success or failure in previously diagnosing the disease from which Napoleon died.

Sir Hudson Lowe wrote no book, which is somewhat remarkable in view of his fondness for writing letters and reports. If he had written an apology it is safe to say that it would have been exhaustive and exhausting. His correspondence, orders, etc., are preserved in no less than 147 volumes of documents, ninety of which deal with the St Helena period. William Forsyth used these as the basis for his three-volume defence of Lowe, published in 1853 and still indispensable for those who want first-hand information. A briefer and more objective account of this strange man, probably the most maligned figure in nineteenth-century history, is to be found in R. C. Seaton's *Napoleon's Captivity in Relation to Sir Hudson Lowe* (1903).

Is it altogether strange that the book just mentioned should be almost the only one to do justice to the governor? It is outside the scope of this study to examine into the reasons for the campaign, to a large extent systematic and carefully planned, which has made the name of Hudson Lowe a synonym for arrogance and cruelty and in the very least for stupidity and tactlessness. The Napoleonic legend required it, of course, just as it also required the growing exaltation of Napoleon's character throughout these six years. Says A. L. Guérard:[1] 'The tradition of his "martyrdom," although disproved, lingers even today in popular imagination. The actual record of his petty warfare with Hudson Lowe affords no pleasant reading. If the British official cannot be absolved of unnecessary punctiliousness, the prisoner shows himself even more deficient in magnanimity. The selfish and histrionic elements in his nature appear nakedly.'

It was the function of the commissioners to watch and report on the English jailers quite as much as on the French prisoners. They should have been, then, from this unique position, well fitted to draw the line between these two extreme positions. The Russian was so fitted by temperament, education, and experience; his Austrian and French colleagues were not. That the reports of Count Balmain are infinitely superior in value and interest is agreed by all those who have been able to compare the three. 'Balmain's reports,' says Philippe Gonnard,[2] 'are very witty and interesting. [Witty, perhaps. They are certainly vivid and readable, and he took vast pains to make them so because he knew his emperor read them carefully.] Those of Stürmer are much less so. Montchenu's are at times ridiculous and at times amusing.' Lord Rosebery in *The Last Phase* goes further and says of Balmain: 'He is accomplished and writes well. Obliging, amiable, and unpretentious, he is beloved by all who know him. He is thus a striking contrast with M. de Montchenu.' Norwood Young writes: 'Balmain was a man of ability, tact, and good sense. He had also a quality which was very precious and singularly rare at St Helena, a sense of humour. His reports were read with interest and pleasure at the Russian court.'[3]

The reports of all three commissioners are well worth reading on their own account, despite the fact that what they tell of Napoleon must be second-hand, chiefly for what they disclose of the character of Sir Hudson Lowe and of the French exiles. They should be honest witnesses, and perhaps the only objective witnesses, provided they lived up to the spirit of their instructions. This they all, at least in the beginning, tried to do. If they had any prejudice it would favour Lowe, since they represented governments which had constituted Napoleon the outlaw of Europe. This would be truest of the French commissioner; and yet his position was a curious one, for, royalist and reactionary as he was, he could not forget that he was a Frenchman, and whatever the feelings of an émigré were toward Napoleon the usurper, he might well prefer the company of his compatriots to that of the ungracious and surly governor.

What the presence of not only Montchenu but Stürmer and Balmain added to the responsibilities and difficulties of Lowe can be more easily surmised than described. The commissioners did not like each other; they did not like Lowe; their duty forbade them from liking the inmates of Longwood. What wonder that they spent their time, imitating in this the French exiles, with mutual recriminations, back-stairs gossip, gambling, and general idling? For the commissioners and the exiles this spying and counter-spying was at least a method of passing the weary hours. For the governor it meant untold anxiety and quarrels and inevitable loss of reputation.

The commissioners, finding their freedom curtailed and their actions sometimes suspected, were naturally inclined to reciprocate by complaining of the governor, and in minor ways were not averse to evading the rules drawn up for the conduct of all residents of the island. Lowe naturally remonstrates; they give him an increasingly bad character in their reports—at least until a year before the end; and the moral influence of the supposedly impartial agents of the powers tells heavily against the harassed governor.

The commissioners should have been withdrawn, maintain most impartial writers (notably Young), when they had achieved the object of their appearance, which was to make it clear that Napoleon was the prisoner of the powers and not of anyone power, to give England moral support, to test the character of Hudson Lowe, and to ascertain that the conditions of the detention were suitable as regards the security and the comfort of the illustrious prisoner. To remain on indefinitely was merely to keep up the semblance of suspicion of the British governor and of the British government, when no such sentiment was entertained. The effect of their presence on Napoleon was of course just as unsatisfactory and lamentable, from his point of view, as it was on Lowe from his. Napoleon realized to the full the international sanction which they gave to his captivity, and while keeping up in public a brave and defiant front, in private he was tremendously depressed by their presence. There seemed now to be no hope whatever of a return to Europe except as the result of some great political upheaval in England, some unusually great piece of stupidity on the part of the Bourbons, or a change of heart in the mystical and impressionable czar.

2

The French commissioner, the Marquis de Montchenu, has been thoroughly described, once and for all, by Frédéric Masson in Volume II of *Autour de Sainte-Hélène*, and some of Masson's characterizations merit citation in a book where their subject appears so often and generally so unfavourably. He belonged to an ancient and distinguished family, and his army service included some years in the King's Horse Guards, from which he had retired in 1785. In 1792 he emigrated, and he used to say concerning the Corsican usurper, 'When this man has fallen I shall petition the king my master to make me his jailer'; and it seems to have become such an obsession with him as to drive the king and Talleyrand to granting the petition simply to rid themselves of his presence. In vain they tried to give him a ministerial post in the diplomatic service; his age, his rank, his family, his devotion to the Bourbons, all warranted the position on which he had set his heart. Accordingly Talleyrand's last official act as minister was to sign the appointment of a man who he knew would be as distasteful to Napoleon as any who could have been chosen. Montchenu's correspondence confirms this guess. His official reports were of course written in phraseology of some dignity, but on his arrival at the island he wrote a circular letter to some of his friends which reeks with pomposity and arrogance. For instance: 'Bonaparte does nothing that I do not know of the instant after; so reassure yourselves, my good compatriots, you will never see him again, I shall answer for it.' The marquis considered himself less the king's commissioner than the agent of the whole Royalist party, charged by them as much as by Louis XVIII with watching *le petit monstre*.

He was regarded by the English as a buffoon. With his absurd boasting, his strange gallantry (this 'gentleman' of sixty sent a love-letter to Lady Lowe), his airs and graces, he was a caricature of the *ancien régime*. The English sailors called him 'old munch-enough' from his hearty appetite. Modern slang would call him a sponge, and his habit of accepting but not sending any invitations to dinners or soirées earned him the name of 'Marquis de Montez-chez-nous.' He was, of course, too anxious to make an impression to care much about the method of doing it, and in this connection the following letter from his secretary, Captain de Gors, to the prime minister, throws some light on both the French and the Russian commissioner: 'I am sorry to say this about M. de Montchenu, but it is my duty to state that all the assertions he has made about his two colleagues are not very well founded and are too great a reflection of his personality. He should have shown himself more just and impartial toward Count Balmain, the only one who really has at heart the common interests of our duty, to which, through excess of zeal, he has sacrificed his rest and his health. M. de Montchenu should not have forgotten that it is to the Count that our mission owes anything interesting that it may have provided; he has never been able to make up his mind to pay, like the latter, a simple visit to the inhabitants of Longwood.'

What were his relations with Lowe? The governor characterizes the Frenchman much more wittily than one would suspect; moreover in very much the sort of language which has been used in speaking of himself. 'The French Marquis, who has been an émigré for thirty years,' he wrote to Sir Henry Bunbury, 'says that it was the people of intelligence [*esprit*] who caused the Revolution. Evidently he didn't take any part in it.' Nevertheless Lowe's relations with Montchenu were more satisfactory than with the other two, because the former spoke no English and was without political or diplomatic training, while his colleagues were both men of large practical experience, men of the world, a good deal of which they had seen, and masters of several languages—in short, men capable of getting their own information and sufficiently imbued with the dignity of their mission and the greatness of the sovereigns whom they represented not to tolerate the position of inferiority in which the governor had made up his mind to place them. Montchenu acquired from Lowe nearly all that he knew: consequently Montchenu's reports present rather a contrast to the others in his estimate of the governor. He was the only commissioner who stayed until the end of the captivity; and while that fact has its historical value, it also adds something to our estimate of his character to know that he refused to leave while the usurper was alive. He took a prominent part at the funeral.

The diplomatic experience of the Austrian commissioner included some years in the legation at Constantinople, from which training it may perhaps be supposed that he had acquired some knowledge of intrigue and finesse which might stand him in good stead in the St Helena atmosphere. His diplomatic training seemed to warrant him in supposing that he had an unusually important rule, and Metternich had to remind him that his quality as commissioner gave him no diplomatic standing. In 1815 he had married the very young daughter of a minor official in the French Ministry of War, who had used his spare time in teaching various elementary subjects to young Las Cases. One can see how this curious fact will give rise to various gossip after Stürmer is ordered to St Helena. When the couple arrived there, Las Cases tried, of course, to renew the acquaintance and to give it a political turn by establishing secret relations with the Austrian commissioner which would enable him to communicate with Europe. The baroness, however, did not lend herself to the attempt, and this intrigue, for once, ended before it began. It did not add to Lowe's happiness to know that Stürmer's wife was French and a great admirer of Napoleon.

Stürmer was, in general, unreasonably hostile to the governor, and the difficulty of their relations, when reported to Vienna, and emphasized by his attempt to deceive Lowe in the Welle affair, brought about his recall in

July, 1818. No successor was appointed, the presence of commissioners being now admitted to be a mistake.

Alexandre Antonovich, Comte de Balmain, was descended from a Scotch family, the Ramsays of Balmain, which had left Scotland in 1685 and emigrated to Russia. His father had occupied the high post of governor-general of the Kursk Government. In 1801, aged twenty but already a captain, Balmain was dismissed from his cavalry regiment for having struck a policeman in a street row, but, restored to imperial favour a few days afterward when Alexander so suddenly came to the throne, he elected for the diplomatic service. There is where, no doubt, he belonged, for he was clever, somewhat unscrupulous, ambitious, fond of society, which soon became fond of him. During his missions at Naples, Vienna, and London, he did very little work, but already, in his fourth decade, he felt physically tired out from the occupations of a homeless, idle, diplomatic career, and morally from his elegant, easy-going scepticism. It was rather becoming to him, and he seems to have increased the pose; for one thing, he knew that it pleased women.

In 1813 he re-entered the army and saw active service culminating at Waterloo. As a reward he was offered the post of commissioner to St Helena. Says Aldanov:[4] 'Count de Balmain had known most of the celebrated people of Europe, and in his collection there was only wanting the most celebrated man of them all. Alexandre Antonovich enjoyed in anticipation the pleasure he would have from his intimate conversations with that genius and also the stories he would afterwards be able to relate. He reckoned that in two or three years he would be able to return to Europe surrounded by an aureole as the chosen friend of the Emperor.'

The instructions drawn up for his guidance (quoted in these reports) were somewhat different from those of his two colleagues, and the latitude allowed him gives the clue to the superior value of his services. His instructions did not place him at variance either with the governor or with the emperor, because he was not directed to 'assure himself with his own eyes' of the latter's existence, and hence did not stultify himself or his mission when he failed ever to see Napoleon.

Moreover he had at least one very good reason for getting to know the governor better, perhaps, than anyone else on the island. In 1816 Sir Hudson Lowe was forty-seven years of age. He was born, incidentally, in the year which also saw the birth of Napoleon, Wellington, Castlereagh, and Marshals Ney, Lannes, and Soult, a combination of friends and antagonists which must be unique. While an ensign in his father's regiment, stationed for some years at Gibraltar, he took occasion to learn French, Spanish, and Italian, and his knowledge of the last he perfected by further study in Italy, so that he would have been able to speak it colloquially with his captive if their relations had been more pleasant. He studied also the Corsican dialect a little later; this man of action was very fond of reading and study.

Several coincidences link him with Napoleonic history. Two years, 1794–96, he spent in Corsica with his regiment before the victories in Italy of the great Corsican forced the British to abandon the island; and he became familiar with the Corsican character. The second coincidence connects him with Elba, where his regiment was next ordered. His best known service up to 1814 was as commander of the Corsican Rangers, which he organized on the island of Minorca from Corsican emigrants who had become dissatisfied with the French régime. For several years Colonel Lowe and his corps saw active service at several points on the Mediterranean. In 1813 he was attached to Blücher, and throughout the campaign of France served him in the important capacity of what would today be termed chief liaison officer. As a reward he was permitted to take the news of Napoleon's abdication to England, and on his arrival was knighted and promoted major-general. In the campaign of Waterloo he was Wellington's quartermaster-general, although Wellington disliked him. The Duke of Wellington assumed command in the Netherlands early in April 1815, and Lowe remained for a few weeks under him as his quartermaster-general, but he was condemned by the duke as a 'damned old fool' for hesitant map-reading and was replaced in May by Colonel Sir William Howe de Lancey.

This summary of his career is given to show that he really had many qualifications for his post at St Helena: his high military rank and knighthood, his success as governor of various other islands, his intimate knowledge of Corsica, his perfect use of both Italian and French, and his acquaintance with many of the foremost celebrities of the day. He was in addition known to be conscientious, determined, and absolutely impervious to political influence of any character and from any direction— qualities which were considered to outweigh the absence of those personal graces which would have made his task so much easier. Let us turn now to his family.

He had married, a few weeks before sailing for St Helena, a widow, whose first husband had been Colonel Johnson, eldest son of Sir John Johnson of Montreal. Opinions differ a great deal about Lady Lowe. Two estimates are quoted in notes to this volume which show that some of those who knew her well admired her; but others did not, and have put on record that she was difficult to get on with, not because, like her husband, she did not know how to be agreeable, but because she imagined that her position required haughtiness. The point is not important because she does not figure conspicuously in this volume. At Colonel Johnson's death in 1812 she was left with two daughters, Charlotte and Susanna, the former of whom was at the time of the family's arrival on the island about thirteen years of age. Susanna died unmarried in 1828; but the elder, in March, 1820, to the surprise of everyone, including the mild surprise of the bridegroom himself, married Alexandre Antonovich de Balmain, who was then about forty-two years old.[5] The match proved not happier than most marriages which are brought about by propinquity and boredom rather than similarity of tastes. After their departure from St Helena the count, of course, found himself back again in the world of society, to which he tried to introduce his girl-bride totally without experience and sophistication and almost without education. She seems to have sometimes exasperated and sometimes amused the court of St Petersburg; she died in 1824.

The question which these personal details raise is, how far did Balmain's courtship hamper him in the expression of his opinions? If one can judge by a perusal of the reports of 1819 and 1820, the answer is, not at all. If one can say that there was a change of attitude toward Lowe, it was not peculiar to him; and if there was any, it was most gradual and, it will be seen, was caused entirely by extraneous factors. His reports make no mention of his marriage. His intimacy with the Lowe family, however, must have some little historical value, whether apparent here or not, in giving him opportunities open to no one else.

NOTE ON THE MANUSCRIPT

The reader, if somewhat new to the literature of the captivity, must not imagine that all these reports present matter which is here given for the first time. Some of the conversations and anecdotes are well known, and if a few of them are again quoted here it is only because they bulk so large in Balmain's mind or because they seem necessary for the context or the interest. The criticism may be made that Stürmer's reports contain some things identical in language with those here given. Although the Russian in one or two cases acknowledges his indebtedness to his colleague for allowing him to use his reports, the reverse is also true. One of Balmain's best estimates of Lowe, for example, is repeated by Stürmer without giving credit; in this as in other cases, Balmain's report is the earlier.

The reports from which this translation has been made are contained in three huge volumes, in which they are written in Balmain's hand, as, unlike Montchenu, he had no secretary. They are in French with the exception of communications from Lowe and other English officers, notably O'Meara, which are copied from the English; however, very few of these are here given, as they can be found elsewhere without great difficulty. Not all of Balmain's reports are used for this book, and the less important are either summarized or entirely omitted.

All the notes are by the editor with the exception of those whose indices are letters of the alphabet, and these are Balmain's. In preparing the notes the editor has made considerable use of Arnold Chaplin's *A St Helena Who's Who* and of Norwood Young's *Napoleon in Exile*, and has glanced through many other works both first-hand and secondary.

THE YEAR 1816

My Instructions

The Powers of Europe having settled by common agreement that Bonaparte should be sent to St Helena and kept on that island under the surveillance and responsibility of England, they agreed that each of them should have the power to place a Commissioner there. The Emperor has chosen you to fulfil this mission, and his Majesty hopes that you will justify, by the zeal and intelligence with which you will acquit yourself of it, the confidence which he shows you on this occasion. Accordingly, you will proceed from here to London and you will place yourself in agreement with the English authorities, under the auspices of Count Liéven, as to the means of securing transportation to your new destination. It is under the immediate orders of that Ambassador that it is his Majesty's intention that you should place yourself. Accordingly, you will follow in their entirety the directions which he will give you henceforth, and in particular those which will be necessitated by the arrangements which he will make toward you with the English Cabinet. On my side I shall be able to give you only a few general observations on the manner in which your mission should be carried out. It is by no means to increase the means of surveillance and still less to control those which England will take that the Powers have decided to send the Commissioners. In this respect our confidence in the loyalty of the British Government must be complete, and it is not to be doubted that the intervention of several agents of other Powers, far from facilitating and enforcing measures of safety, would only serve to complicate them and might even compromise them. It is England which is charged with the whole responsibility. It is then to her that we must leave the choice of means which she will judge necessary in this connection. However, a European significance has been given to this whole affair in making Bonaparte the prisoner of Europe, and it is on that account that the idea has been conceived of sending to St Helena Commissioners from each Power. In order to conform to the motives which I have just laid before you, you will then avoid carefully the appearance of intervening and of making pronouncements on the measures which the English Government and authorities will take. Your rôle will be purely passive. You will observe all and render an account of all. You will bring to bear in your relations with the English officials a spirit of conciliation in keeping with the bonds of alliance and friendship uniting the two Courts. In your relations with Bonaparte you will observe that discretion and moderation required by a situation so delicate and that personal respect which is due to him.[6] You will neither avoid nor seek occasions to see him, and in that respect you will conform strictly to the rules which will be established by the Governor. But you will note daily all that you may learn of him and you will specially apply yourself to write the salient features of his conversations either with you or with the Commissioners of other Powers, or with other people. An accurate journal kept up with care and regularity cannot fail to offer to history material of great value. *However, never must that consideration encourage you to deviate from the way which is traced out for you above.* You will address your reports to the Ministry of Foreign Affairs and they will be forwarded through Count Liéven. His Majesty the Emperor has deigned to award you a salary of 1200 pounds sterling, together with 2000 ducats for the expenses of your voyage and establishment. You will receive herewith the copy of your ukase relative to this beneficent grant.

NESSELRODE.[7]

Paris, 18/30 September, 1815.[8]

(Here follows ukase in Russian)[9]

Instructions of Count Liéven

His Imperial Majesty in informing me of your destination, the island of St Helena, and the relations which will result between you and the Emperor's Ambassador at London, has asked me to supplement the instructions with which you have previously been provided by such others as my relations with the British Government may cause me to judge useful to you at the post to which you are about to proceed.

I cannot better follow the instructions of his Majesty the Emperor in regard to the task laid down for you than by making your instructions a subject of frank deliberation with the Secretary of State for the Colonies. It is important for you, Monsieur le Comte, to know that Lord

Bathurst was pleased to express to me his entire assent in respect to the rules it has been enjoined upon you to follow. This circumstance should increase still further, if possible, your anxiety to conform strictly to the directions which have been given to you in regard to your relations with the Governor of the island as well as with Bonaparte; and by deserving the confidence of the former you will be sure faithfully to fulfil the task which has been confided to you. I recommend to you, especially in view of the very judicious observations of my Lord Bathurst, not to deviate in your personal relations to Bonaparte from the rule which is prescribed for you by our court, and according to which these relations should be maintained only with the knowledge of the Governor.

There is one point which the Secretary of State has desired that I mention to you particularly: It is not impossible that during your stay at St Helena chance may cause you to notice some involuntary omission in the measures established to guard the person of Bonaparte. In such a case I am requested by the British Government to ask you to communicate frankly your observations to the Governor of the island. . . .

LIÉVEN.

London, 15/27 March, 1816.

My Reports to Count Nesselrode

No. 1

London, 19 March, 1816.

At last I have the honour of informing your Excellency that I am on the point of embarking for my destination. The frigate *New Castle* has just entered the harbour of Portsmouth, prepared to receive the foreign Commissioners and to take them to St Helena; where that vessel is to replace the *Northumberland*, which returns to England. I am at this moment terminating with Baron Stürmer some unimportant arrangements, after which we await before setting sail only the Marquis de Montchenu, French Commissioner, whose departure from Paris has been delayed a few days.

Permit me to profit by this occasion to make a representation which costs my dignity much, especially in the gratitude which I have for the numberless benefits which his Majesty the Emperor has already shown me, but which is indispensable because it concerns the dignity of his service. I have always believed that the funds which had been granted me for my establishment and those assigned for its maintenance were more than sufficient to enable me to live properly at St Helena. However, having secured the most exact and substantial information on this point, having at different intervals questioned both General Beatson, the last Governor of the island, and Sir Hudson Lowe, the present Governor, and twenty other people, all of whom have been on the spot, I am assured in the most positive manner that these means, ample as they may appear, do not correspond to the cost of living in the country, nor to the quantity of objects with which it is necessary to be provided on arriving. In spite of this certainty which I have been acquiring for a long time, I have not wished to make it an object of special report to your Excellency before the other two Commissioners have asked and obtained relief. Baron Stürmer has been the first to make a request at his Court. What he learned about St Helena made him so dissatisfied over his fate that, profiting by the long delay preventing our speedy departure, he proceeded to Milan to see Count Metternich with the enclosed memorandum from General Beatson and a despatch from Count Esterházy to support him. His trip has had the desired effect. His representations were deemed well founded, and he has returned to London provided with the German document, a copy of which I take the liberty to enclose herewith. By this you will see, Monsieur le Comte, that if it is proposed to regulate the definitive allowance of Baron Stürmer according to what he will communicate regarding the prices at St Helena, he will in the meantime be given the means to meet his expenses—and that is, as a matter of fact, the only fitting arrangement in cases which cannot be supported by precedent. As for the Marquis de Montchenu, the Duc de Richelieu has only been waiting for this decision of the Emperor of Austria in order to assure him of the same advantages. As a consequence of all these circumstances, I believe, it is only my duty to beg your Excellency to emphasize to his Majesty the Emperor the difficulties of the position that I occupy. I have been obliged, in order to suffice for the supply of provisions and endless purchases which I have had to make, to leave in London a third of my salary, and it is with only the other two thirds that I am going to struggle at St Helena against all that may happen. You will understand, Monsieur le Comte, how I shall suffer as a Russian officer in cutting such a sad figure before the English functionaries. That it is which causes me to hope your Excellency will deign to interest himself in my favour and will not delay in rescuing me from a painful uncertainty.

I have the honour to be, etc.

[COPY]
Memorandum for His Excellency Monseigneur le Prince Esterházy

It seems to me that the august Sovereigns of Europe, when naming Commissioners for the island of St Helena, were not aware of the inconveniences, the very heavy expenses, and the privations to which the latter would be exposed.

One of the greatest difficulties to which they will be subjected at first will be to find proper quarters on account of the small size of the city of St James, which contains scarcely thirty adequate houses, even they being occupied in great part at this moment by the civil and military employees of the East India Company and by natives of the island.

If any of these houses were for rent it could scarcely be had for less than *two or three hundred pounds sterling a year, of course entirely unprovided with furniture.* Moreover it is probable that such houses will be rented by officers of the troops which are to form the new garrison of the island. It is true that there are some houses belonging to the lower class where travellers are received coming from India, but living is much dearer there than in the most expensive hotels of London. A master, man or woman, pays thirty shillings a day for board and lodging; a servant of either sex, and even down to the smallest child, fifteen shillings a day. Furthermore, it is reasonable to believe that such an arrangement would scarcely be fitting to the rank and position of an Imperial or Royal Commissioner. Foreseeing all these inconveniences, I suggested four months ago to Lord Buckinghamshire, Secretary of State for the Indies, to send to St Helena a considerable quantity of timber in order to have houses built of all sizes.

Another subject which should be taken into consideration is the high cost of the products of the island. During the last twelve to fifteen years, in 1811, the prices were as follows:

Beef	14	pence a pound	
Pork	15	*ditto*	
Flour and Bread	5	*ditto*	
Meat of the smallest kind	40–60	shillings	
A duck and a chicken	7–12	*ditto*	
A goose	21–25	*ditto*	
Turkey	32–42	*ditto*	
Potatoes	10–12	*ditto*	per bushel
Hay	10–12	*ditto*	per hundredweight
Eggs	3–4	*ditto*	*per dozen*

It appears probable, not to say certain, that the increase of the garrison, the presence of naval forces, and the crowd of newcomers, as a result of the new importance which has just been given to the island, will cause the prices of all these articles to rise to a point where they have never been before. These details will show how necessary it is to proportion the allowances of the Commissioners according to the expenses to which they must be subjected.

It is presumed that their Sovereigns will not care to put them in a position inferior to that of the Lieutenant-Governor of the island, who is only a Lieutenant-Colonel in the army and who has besides a considerable allowance, a town house, and another in the country, to which is added a garden of 200 acres for the pasturing of cows, oxen, and sheep for his exclusive use. Besides all these advantages, which are inconsiderable in a country offering so little resources by itself, he has an establishment of slaves and two houses kept up at the expense of the East India Company. As for the privations which the Commissioners will have to experience, they are too numerous to mention. They consist of the lack of all comforts of social life which are so easily procured in Europe. To sacrifice them, as will become necessary, will seriously affect their diet, which will be very different from that to which they are accustomed. Only rarely will they have any fresh meat and they must very often live upon fish and salt meat.

London, 26 December, 1815.

ALEX. BEATSON,
Former Governor of the Island of St Helena.[10]

No. 2
St Helena, June 18, 1816, by the *Northumberland*, ship of the line, Admiral Cockburn.

I am setting foot at this moment on the island of St Helena. We have arrived there after a voyage of seven weeks. Admiral Cockburn,[11] who has just been replaced in his command by Admiral Malcolm,[12] is so anxious to return to London that I can scarcely give your Excellency any other news. He must leave tomorrow at sunrise. At the end of this week a vessel from India will set sail for Europe. I hope then to have interesting details to communicate.

I have the honour to be, etc.

No. 3
June 29, 1816.
An English brig, the *Hecate*, has reached us this morning from the Cape of Good Hope, and her departure has just been announced for tomorrow

after midnight. I give myself the pleasure of profiting by this occasion to write your Excellency, but I beg you to content yourself today with a very imperfect report. I have as yet had only the chance to put myself in touch with the Governor and to give the most superficial glance at my surroundings.

As it is scarcely possible to give a description of St Helena other than that already well known in Europe, I content myself with repeating that it seems to me to be that spot in the world which is the saddest, the most isolated, the most unapproachable, the easiest to defend, the hardest to attack, the most unsociable, the poorest, the dearest, and especially the most appropriate for the use to which it is now put. Such is the general idea which one must have of it. Any attempt against the island would be pure madness. I believe that I can already assure you of that. Nature has contributed the first and the greatest obstacles, and the English Governor does not cease to add to the means of defence, the greater part of which seems unnecessary. Three regiments of infantry, five companies of artillery, a detachment of dragoons for the service of a rather considerable staff, form the extent of the garrison. Two frigates, one of them of 50 guns, some brigs and sloops guard the sea, and the number of cannon disposable on the coasts and the interior of the country is striking. Sir Hudson Lowe is to give me soon an exact report of his troops as well as the military plan of the island. I shall hasten to enclose them in my next report. The strictest discipline is established at all points for the direct and indirect surveillance of Bonaparte. In the daytime walking in certain spots is permitted only with a passport from the Governor. At night one can go nowhere without the countersign. In some directions wherever we turn we see only sentinels, guards, and patrols. The ex-Emperor occupies the pavilion of the Lieutenant-Governor, known as Longwood; a territory of several miles in circumference is at his disposal, which he uses with perfect freedom. The guard approaches it only after he has retired and watches over the house until the next day. If he wishes to pass that barrier, always lined with troops and defended by a park of artillery, he is followed by an officer who never loses him from sight. Those who wish to enter, no matter how or why, must be provided with an extraordinary permit. On sea the regulations are still stricter. The day when our vessel appeared before the port of St James one of the batteries of the fort fired upon it, using a 24-pound ball, because Admiral Malcolm had failed to despatch someone to the island to announce his arrival. No vessel after the evening gun may leave or shift its position. There are officers charged exclusively with that duty during the night. This state of things has deprived St Helena of an important means of livelihood—fishing. It now carries on that occupation only by day and fish is becoming as scarce as fresh meat.

I have no desire, Monsieur le Comte, to venture opinions on these measures of safety, but I acknowledge I experience some difficulty in realizing their real necessity. An island detached from the rest of the world, to which access is gained only by a single wind, where one enters only by a single side, where the rocks are piled one upon another, forming precipices at each step, could, it seems to me, be guarded efficiently at much less expense.

I am going now to speak to your Excellency of Bonaparte himself. His mental dispositions are sufficiently variable. Most frequently he shows some temper, but physically he in no way reveals his mental disturbance. He is always in good health and promises to live a long time. As yet nobody has been able to discover whether he is resigned to his fate or whether he entertains hopes. It is said that he bases any hope of leaving the island on the English Opposition. What can be safely said is that he continually protests against his arrest and has himself treated at Longwood as Emperor. Bertrand, Montholon, Las Cases, Gourgaud, and all his suite render him, as ever, the highest honours. He ordinarily receives strangers who ask to see him, but he offers neither meals nor entertainments, and never goes out of his bounds. The presence of an English officer who has to accompany him annoys him and causes him to suffer. For the same reason he avoids in his walks the guards and sentinels. He rises at noon, breakfasts, busies himself in his house with different things until three o'clock; at four receives people who are announced to him, then takes a walk or drives in a six-horse carriage; rarely rides horseback, dines at eight, remains at table only three quarters of an hour, plays his game of *reversis*, goes to bed, and gets up in the night at different times to work. He is writing his history with the help of the 'Moniteur.' He is also learning English. His conversation would be interesting if you could follow it, for he occasionally lets himself go in the old imperial manner; but ordinarily he sees only his French people, and the inconsequential things which he says to the English, except perhaps to Admiral Cockburn, are either distorted by the national vanity or prove nothing. General Lowe treats him with all possible respect and even lends himself in some degree to the imperial pose. Yet he does not like Lowe and has seen him only three or four times. He seems somewhat to prefer Admiral Malcolm, who plays to perfection the 'good child' but does not deviate more than the other from the path mapped out for him.[13] I will add as a rather curious circumstance that he has definitely put away his uniform and wears a hunting coat. I flatter myself, Monsieur le Comte, on being able soon to send you a more interesting report.

I have the honour to be, etc.

No. 4

June 29, 1816.

In order not to lengthen unduly my first report, I included therein only a few details relative to Bonaparte. The object of the present report will be to inform your Excellency of what concerns me directly as Commissioner. I can only congratulate myself for the reception given to us both on board the *New Castle* and at St Helena, as well as for the continual attention paid us by the English authorities. Sir Hudson Lowe immediately showed me a confidence which singularly attracted me. On my side I explained to him without delay the object of my mission, and our relations were thus quite naturally established. He has obligated himself to keep me constantly in touch with the news of the island and especially with what is happening at Longwood. The two other Commissioners had positive orders to assure themselves by their own eyes of the existence of Bonaparte and to draw up a monthly report countersigned by the Governor. Negotiations to this effect were opened with Marshal Bertrand. The ex-Emperor asked if we bore him letters from our Sovereigns. When he realized for what purpose we wished to see him, he declaimed violently against the conference of the 2nd of August, and there the thing stayed. The matter was rather embarrassing for everybody. The Marquis de Montchenu and Baron von Stürmer, according to their instructions, were to show no particular respect toward Bonaparte, and General Lowe was reluctant to force his door. The gentlemen then thought fit to address to Lowe a note from all the Commissioners in order that his refusal might be made official, and hence might be used to justify them in the eyes of their court. As my instructions were not particular in this respect, and as, moreover, I saw a marked opposition on the part of Sir Hudson Lowe, and since without humiliating uselessly the prisoner of Europe, I could meet him every day and satisfy myself in this affair, I refused to join them in that attempt which is not only detrimental to the personal respect owed to him, but would be something that neither the Governor nor the Admiral would ever permit.

I have the honour to be, etc.

No. 5

September 6, 1816.

If my duty at St Helena is confined to satisfying myself as an eye-witness of the existence of Bonaparte and to report on what is happening outside of his house, I find no difficulties in fulfilling it. Sir Hudson Lowe has opened to me all the paths on the island and that of Longwood up to his prisoner's door. But if your Excellency expects, as you justifiably may, an interesting journal which may one day serve as a guide to history, I fear that I can inadequately answer your expectations. Napoleon has laid down the principle of no longer going out of his bounds, of seeing people only in passing, and of keeping up the imperial pose. As long as this manner of conducting himself lasts, I can neither listen to him often nor interrogate him, nor observe him nearby, and my correspondence regarding him will be only a pastime.

What has struck me from the moment of my arrival (though it is rather natural) is the enormous ascendancy which this man, surrounded by guards, by rocks, by precipices, still keeps over men's minds. Everything at St Helena reflects his superiority. The French tremble at his look and deem themselves only too happy to serve him. Las Cases says to whoever wishes to hear him, 'My happiness consists in contemplating a hero, a prodigy.' The English approach him now only with timidity. Even those who guard him solicit a look, an interview, a word. Nobody dares to treat him as an equal. His genius, which in this abasement of fortune can fix itself on nothing great, amuses itself in vexing people. He excites the envy of some, while flattering others. He is gracious toward his associates and wishes to humiliate those above him. He makes much of the Admiral and communicates with the Governor through Bertrand. It is now apparent that he is trying to embroil various people and to sow dissension everywhere. To me this conduct seems only a gratuitous spitefulness. Perhaps it is part of a well thought out design of which he alone possesses the secret, but I do not see that anything can be done to remedy it.

Bonaparte, before being confided to Sir George Cockburn, was rather pliant. It even appears that at that time he had no idea of sequestering himself as he has since done. This Admiral, through his badly applied zeal or rather perhaps to secure some prestige from it for himself, has, as it were, scared him. The latter had the idea that he could establish himself at Longwood on a footing of perfect equality. He seated himself in the imperial presence and in his bedroom without having been asked. He frequently contradicted him and drove him to his present extremity. From this there resulted disputes, sulkiness, a continual embarrassment between them; finally open rupture, which was the end of Cockburn, for, having one day presented himself with someone to see the ex-Emperor, the door was closed upon him and the companion entered. After this affront they no longer saw each other. The Admiral has left without saying goodbye. His presence in Europe may give another complexion to these statements, but I guarantee them such as I report them. It is a fact that Sir George Cockburn, who in many ways possesses much merit, has shown too much freedom in this affair, lacking tact in allowing no distinction between Bonaparte and himself, lacking delicacy in treating him bluntly on board his vessel, lacking generosity in allowing him no individuality, in trying in almost everything to pre-judge his character. It was while speaking of him that the illustrious prisoner said one day that they were putting chains on him but that they should pay him the respect which was due him. Such examples are not repeated often with a mind of his calibre, so that nobody since that time has again made that mistake. Sir Pulteney Malcolm, not less ambitious than Admiral Cockburn, but more clever and with a more supple character, at first felt that it was necessary to take another kind of beginning. In order to see Napoleon he would have had to go to Count Bertrand, and to Madame Bertrand to present to her Lady, Malcolm. This attempt naturally biased the prisoner in his favour. From his very first visit he had it understood that the surveillance of the prisoner in no way concerned him, and that only the sea, up to the Île de France belonged to him. It was merely another means of pleasing Napoleon. He has been exceedingly modest and quite a lady's man, so that his tactics have succeeded and he is today a favourite. He is sought out, he is flattered; interviews are sought with him lasting entire hours. As a matter of fact this predilection has for its real object only to seduce him or to mystify other people. But the Admiral is not the man to make a mistake. He profits by it because he is inquisitive and is thinking of writing his memoirs. He enjoys it all because it gives him relaxation. His conduct is assuredly on a higher plane than that of his predecessor.

Sir Hudson Lowe is not successful in the same way. He tries to satisfy Bonaparte. He treats him with respect and ceremony, does not complain of his brusque manner, tolerates his caprices, in short achieves the impossible. But he will never be anything except his scourge. There is too much incompatibility between the two men. The mind of the one is still restless. He is a wandering genius who, in the circumstance where fate has reduced him, wishes to take his flight and seeks perhaps to make converts for himself. The other opposes to this strong will merely an inexhaustible fund of commonplace ideas and a cold suspicious nature, a repulsive exterior with, however, the best intentions in the world, and a tyrannical precision in fulfilling his duty. To sum up, he who knows only how to command is at the mercy of him who knows only how to obey. Hence, there is no manner of displeasing his jailer which the prisoner has not tried. Of this I shall cite only a few of the most remarkable instances. The wife of Lord Moira on her way to India stopped at St Helena. She had, like everybody, a desire to see Bonaparte. Sir Hudson Lowe conceived the idea of having them dine together and consequently wrote to Longwood, but addressed the ex-Emperor as General. The latter never replied to the note of invitation, contenting himself with sending his excuses to Lady Moira.[14]

The officers of the Sixty-sixth Regiment of infantry desired to be presented to Napoleon. Marshal Bertrand fixed the day, and these officers, with their commander at their head, had already assembled waiting for the door to open. I do not know by what chance Sir Pulteney Malcolm, who suspected nothing, arrived at the same hour with his officers from the *New Castle*. The navy was first introduced and the admiral had a very long interview. The army, after having waited the entire morning, retired somewhat confused, and the matter was never reintroduced. Up to now neither the Bertrands nor the Montholons nor anybody at Longwood has had permission to see Lady Lowe, a charming woman who entertains pleasant gatherings at Plantation House.[15] On the other hand, Lady Malcolm, who does not even know French, receives them and returns their visits at any time. Furthermore, Bonaparte has acknowledged his antipathy for Sir Hudson Lowe. Admiral Malcolm reproached him recently for misunderstanding that good man and for not showing him sufficient confidence. 'You are right,' said he; 'it is perhaps a childishness on my part, but we are not masters of our own impressions.' Cockburn's grievances are of another kind. There we have a man of character who first thinks in the large. I should wish Lowe to be like that.

After having given an idea of the principal individuals at St Helena, I will try to satisfy your Excellency's curiosity by giving a rather interesting collection of anecdotes and conversations and other peculiarities of the life of Napoleon.

The Interior of Longwood

Sent to the end of the world as the prisoner of Europe, treated by Cockburn as a comrade, ceaselessly exposed to the not very delicate manners of the English who ever since Waterloo have been without any respect, Bonaparte has necessarily to think of his glory and to maintain the degree of his rank. Therein he succeeded by a very simple means. He shut himself up within his bounds where nobody had the right to control his actions, and became inaccessible. His guards, who were already assuming a tone of familiarity, became surprised at this resolution. Each of them on coming here had formed his own ideas regarding their captive. When they saw at what distance they were held, they forgot all respect, formality, modesty. They went wherever they wanted to go, and the ex-Emperor reappeared in all his majesty. His household today is a court, of which Bertrand is the Grand Marshal; Las Cases, Secretary of State; Montholon, first Maître d'Hôtel; Gourgaud, General Aide-de-Camp; Piontowski, groom; Mmes. Bertrand and Montholon, ladies of honour. Those who wish to be presented to him, to have an interview or to carry on any business whatever, must apply to the Grand Marshal, since application to the Governor means refusal. Lady Moira and other distinguished English people who believed that they could have access to him have never been able to get admitted.

Receptions are not quite the same for everybody. High office, merit, personality, and especially the ideas which one may have on Napoleon, are the measure of one's success in securing admission. There are some whom he likes to see tête-à-tête, some with whom he holds rather long conversations. The other, greater, number is first sent away and then received before the door at the entrance to the garden. Rarely is a second audience granted except to those from whom some advantage may be expected, such as ladies, travellers, etc. He excuses himself on the pretext of indisposition, and in that case further requests are not made. It also happens that the minor officers announced in advance to be presented to him form an antechamber during entire hours and are then put off to another day.

At his audiences Napoleon appears in a green hunting-coat quite well worn, with silver buttons in the shape of stags, wild boars, and foxes; white trousers and stockings with oval buckles of gold. His everyday hat is under his arm. He wears the plaque of the Legion of Honour and carries a snuff-box in his hand. Never does he invite his guests to be seated unless he himself is lying down. He fears lest anyone assume Cockburn's example of self-assurance, which he is careful to prevent by himself always standing. Sir Pulteney Malcolm has had at Longwood interviews lasting three or four hours, during which they finally because of fatigue leaned upon the table or against the wall, and nothing can persuade him to relax on this point. When there are no strangers the etiquette is a little less strict, and Bonaparte becomes more natural. Like a soldier of fortune he is brusque, outspoken, despotic. He throws out gross words without interruption and treats his French people as slaves. He is rather fond of music and has Italian airs sung to him after dinner by Madame de Montholon. She is at present the only one who can give him this diversion. What a contrast for a man who used to dispose of all the orchestras of Paris! Italian is his favourite language. He speaks it with the Governor, with his doctor and all those who know anything of it. He spends his evenings playing cards or chess, but he is not very much interested in any game, and becomes angry when he loses. Gourgaud who knows this weakness makes intentional mistakes in order to let him win. His mornings he spends largely with books. He finds pleasure in reading newspapers and is working with Las Cases on his history. This he is apparently writing in the style of Cæsar's Commentaries and narrates in the third person. Toward four o'clock he walks, with short, quick steps, before his door; sometimes he uses a six-horse carriage, driving at a gallop around his boundaries. Since my arrival he has not gone out on horseback, for this exercise is no longer to his taste. His house of

Longwood without being either large or magnificent is convenient enough and the furniture is all of fine mahogany. He has a garden on the side where Admiral Malcolm has had erected a superb tent. They are willing to build him a pavilion of a more regular architecture, and the island is filled with material for that purpose sent from England. But whether he hopes for some sort of a change in his position or whether he wishes to annoy Sir Hudson Love, no one as yet has been able to persuade him to consent to it. His expenditures are only what the English Government allow him and it is not known whether or not he has private means; since his fall he has said or done nothing which might give any clue. It is supposed, however, that he has some, and that they are placed in England under an assumed name.

His Suite

It is said at St Helena that it is the people around Bonaparte who by their underhanded dealings and the reports which they give him have a bad influence over his character and his conduct in general. This appears to me doubtful. But the fact remains that all of his French people hate each other cordially. Each wishes to be the favourite of the master; hence arise very ridiculous scenes. Montholon,[16] charged with the interior of the palace, is jealous of Bertrand, who has charge of the exterior. Gourgaud,[17] tired of parading in his quality of Aide-de-Camp in an antechamber, views with displeasure the more important occupations of Las Cases.[18] The latter, in order to yield to him in nothing, thinks that in his hours of pleasure he can master the art of horseback riding. A dwarf's stature, an awkward and wheedling manner, do not discourage him from this experiment, for he would break his neck rather than discontinue it. It is in thus blinding themselves to the reality of their position that these unhappy exiles, who would be well thought of if they had any *esprit de corps*, are exciting the ridicule of everybody. Bertrand is a weak but well-meaning man, always melancholy and sometimes in despair. He is the least restless of the band.[19] His wife strongly urged him to establish himself in England in order to be near Paris, but, completely under Bonaparte's will, he has not been able to make up his mind to leave St Helena. Montholon is but a poor specimen. He embarked at Rochefort with his master less through attachment and gratitude than because he was head over heels in debt. At Longwood he believes himself something of a personage and passes for a determined liar. Gourgaud, a nephew of Dugazon, the comedian, is a soldier of fortune, bold and swaggering. He does not mix into the intrigues, but yet he is noisy, gross, and vain. That is all that can be said of him. Las Cases has made for Bonaparte the sacrifice of his liberty without motives of self-interest. This was but a movement of spontaneous generosity; perhaps also there was a desire of leaving to posterity an exact and detailed history of his hero. Whatever inconsistencies there may be in his conduct, he makes up for by his sincerity and devotion. Piontkowski was a simple Polish lancer on the island of Elba. To reward his fidelity Napoleon made him captain and an orderly officer and Chevalier of the Legion of Honour. He is a big gentle fellow of whom nobody complains, and yet he is somewhat looked down upon at Longwood. I cannot imagine what decided him to expatriate himself. Madame Bertrand and Madame Montholon do not like each other, and yet here they are, condemned to live together. The one is imposing and pretty; the other is amiable and a musician.

O'Meara and Poppleton

O'Meara is the secret agent of Sir Hudson Lowe at Longwood.[20] This doctor is a clever and discreet man. He informs Bonaparte of what is said and done on the island in order to have access to him. At the same time he keeps a record of his slightest action and words. Without seeming to do so, he pokes his nose in everywhere, and it is through him that they learn an immense number of details of a character more or less to interest the watchers. Poppleton is a Captain in the Fifty-third Regiment of infantry,[21] sent to Longwood in order to help guard Bonaparte. Accordingly he is lodged near the latter and must see him every day. Morning and evening he gives news of him to the Governor by a system of signals, and if he goes outside of his boundaries, the Captain follows him and never loses sight of him. This poor man, who is acquainted only with his trade of war and has no idea of the amenities of life, is the pet aversion of all the French prisoners.[22]

Conversations

Napoleon speaks often to Sir Pulteney Malcolm of past events. I will put down word for word what the Admiral, who shows me many confidences, has communicated to me of his interviews with him.

Battle of Waterloo:

N. Do you know that Wellington risked too much? He ought to have retired and waited for his allies. Without the Prussians he was beaten.

M. Yes, but the Duke knew that the Prussians would come up.

N. How would he know it? If Grouchy had done his duty we would not have been in that fix. It is he who lost everything.

M. What made you open that campaign by an attack against the Prussians? The English position should have disturbed you more. That was the side of the sea and should have been made sure of.

N. The character of the Generals whom I had at the head of my army traced out for me my conduct. That drunken Hussar,[23] impatient to distinguish himself, would have left everything to succour England. I would have had too many enemies at once. I beat him. I threw his troops into disorder. Grouchy should have prevented him from undertaking anything. My orders were wretchedly executed. But although the Prussians did much, the day belongs to Wellington.

M. What do you think of the Prussians?

N. They are rascals.

M. And their army?

N. It cost me so little to crush it at Jena, with their Potsdam manoeuvres, that I was surprised at my victory.

M. But it has changed since?

N. A little.

Invasion of England:

M. What was the real object of your great preparations at Boulogne?

N. The crossing of the Channel by my soldiers.

M. Then the conquest of England appeared to you easy?

N. No, but it was assuredly worth the trouble of being tried.

M. We were never able to guess your plan.

N. It was simple. My fleet made a feint of going to America with troops for debarkation. I was sure that the greater part of yours would follow it there. Villeneuve, profiting then by the first favourable chance, of which there are so many at sea, was to turn around short, to regain the Channel at least two weeks before the English Admiral, and to cruise there while my transports crossed.

His Imprisonment at St Helena:

N. You are going always to keep me here?

M. I believe so.

N. You have, then, no other colonies?

M. You would not be better off anywhere else.

N. What they are doing at St Helena is absurd, ridiculous. Look here. That soldier on the tip of that rock over there, what good is he? Do you fear that I should escape? Could even a bird escape? I realize that any *city* may well be forbidden to me. That is natural enough, but apart from that, I ought to be free.

M. You are. You are not even prevented from going to town.

N. With that officer [Poppleton] at my heels? That would be to degrade me, to recognize that I am but a prisoner, which I am not.

M. However, we cannot treat you any longer as a Sovereign.

N. And why not? Why not leave me that empty honour? In my position on this rock, what harm can it do?

M. Then we would have to give you your title of Emperor.

N. (*after a moment of reflection.*) No, I have abdicated.

M. You do not wish to be called General?

N. I have not been a General since my return from Egypt. Let me be called simply Napoleon.

The Duke of Enghien:

M. For what crime was the Duke of Enghien tried and executed?

N. Tried! I would not have him tried at all. I had him shot. He was conspiring against me. That was proved.

Other Matters:

Bonaparte speaks rarely of his Russian campaign. One day he said to Admiral Cockburn: 'For my glory I should have died at Moscow.' He learned with indifference of the death of his brother-in-law, Murat. The death of Marshal Ney seemed to affect him more. 'He was beheaded,' he cried. They answered him, no, that he had been shot. 'That is impossible, for it was the Peers who tried him.' Then he made a turn or two around the room and said, 'He was brave, he was brave. Yes, but he betrayed me at Fontainebleau.'[24]

What the English newspapers have published regarding his arguments with Poppleton and regarding the sentinel who aimed a gun at him is false. Here is the truth. Napoleon accompanied by his ordinary retinue was riding horseback. On the way the idea comes to him to examine a cliff. He spurs his horse and goes out of his bounds. Poppleton at the same time starts after him, but being badly mounted he cannot follow and loses sight of the cavalcade. He must have thought that his prisoner was going to swim the ocean and utters loud cries after him. Finally he catches up and begins to reprimand him. One look from Bonaparte cuts short his speech. All that he dares is to say between his teeth, 'The next time, sir, I will take better care.' That is the base on which these fables have been built. When Bonaparte was living with Mr Balcombe he amused himself considerably at the frolics of Miss Betsy, the youngest daughter of his host.[25] He taught her geography. He played blindman's-buff with her and passed his life in a circle of children. One day she asked him who burned Moscow. He answered, striking his fist with his hand, 'It was I.' I often see that charming little girl, but I will not take up further space with the things that she taught me about her friend Bony (for it was thus that she called him), since that would make a volume of gossip. At St Helena as elsewhere Bonaparte took every precaution against night attacks. I am now occupying the apartment where he stayed on the day of his arrival. The door of the bedroom has an English lock, which is almost impossible to force. However, he had put on in addition a large bolt which is still there, and which is pointed out to the curious.

We have not yet been able to see the ex-Emperor. He does not wish to meet the Commissioners. My two colleagues are negotiating on this subject with the Governor. I am awaiting the determination of this strange affair in which I have been quite neutral, in order to make a report on it to your Excellency.

I have the honour to be, etc.

Memorandum of Artillery at St Helena

50 Battery pieces
24 Campaign pieces
Some mortars

Here follows a detailed account of the garrison at St Helena by companies, totalling 2,784 men, together with a list of the squadron under the command of Sir Pulteney Malcolm, showing three frigates, two armed vessels, and six brigs. Here also follows a list, showing the composition of the household of Bonaparte.

No. 6

September 10, 1816.

I had the honour of informing your Excellency by my report numbered 4 of the discussions begun between the Austrian and French Commissioners at the time of their arrival at St Helena. You will see by the present that this account which forms the base of their instructions has produced only arguments of every nature. I shall set forth this affair according to the order of dates. On June 17 at five o'clock in the evening the *New Castle* touched the island. We were immediately advised that the departure of the *Northumberland* was fixed for the nineteenth. The Marquis de Montchenu, wishing to profit by that occasion to send to France his first report, landed the same day and strongly urged the English authorities to take him to Longwood. He was very insistent, saying that the peace of Europe depended upon his request. But it was unanimously rejected, and my colleague returned to sleep on board, a little annoyed at his failure. In the meantime O'Meara informed the French Commissioner of what had happened. 'I know that Montchenu,' cried Napoleon in anger; 'he is an old woman, a gossip, an arm-chair gentleman who has never smelt powder. I shall not see him.' The unfortunate part of this is that the portrait is a true one. On the eighteenth we landed with much ceremony, together with Admiral Malcolm. General de Montchenu was no sooner in the town that he renewed his importunity of the day before. The reasons given for the refusal were the bad temper of Bonaparte, the respect which the British Government had promised him, the impossibility of going so rapidly in an affair of this kind. On the nineteenth Montchenu had the chagrin of witnessing the departure of the *Northumberland* without being able to send his report by her. On the twenty-sixth we discussed the desirability of conferring with the Governor on the real object of our mission and of putting ourselves in touch with him and our staff. Baron Stürmer spoke first and said that his only interest was to assure himself by his own eyes of the existence of the prisoner of Europe and to send a report to his Court every month. The French Commissioner gave the same explanations. As, however, he brought to this conference, according to himself at least, a very high idea of his person and of his post (the only one which he has ever filled), the certainty of playing here a principal part and of exercising his influence over Bonaparte appealed so strongly to him that he made an emphatic speech which lasted a whole hour and tired his audience. Sir Hudson Lowe answered these gentlemen that the Convention of August 2, by virtue of which the Commissioners of the Allied Powers were now at St Helena, had not been transmitted officially to him, but that he would do his best to put them in touch with their Governments. Since my instructions did not prescribe anything in respect to these negotiations, I said little. On the twenty-seventh Sir Hudson Lowe announced to Count Bertrand the arrival of the Commissioners and advised him of our desire to see General Bonaparte. The Grand Marshal, who expected these overtures, made evasive replies. He asked if we had letters from our Sovereigns.

The Marquis de Montchenu disapproved this indirect attempt. 'It is not thus,' he said to me, 'that criminals are treated.' Baron Stürmer took it also as a bad omen, and these gentlemen wrote on this subject a very lively remonstrance to the Governor, which, however, led to nothing. It was then that the question arose for the first time of forcing the door of Longwood, and I refused to sign the note of the Commissioners of which mention is made in my despatch of June 29. On the twenty-eighth and following days we sought the authentic document which Count Bertrand was asking for. Unhappily it was not found, and Sir Hudson Lowe finally took upon himself a direct application to Bonaparte. 'If these gentlemen,' said the latter, 'wish to be presented as individuals there will be no objection, and let them go to the Grand Marshal; if it is as Commissioners, allow me to see the Convention of the second of August and I shall consider it.'

There the affair remained. During these negotiations Admiral Malcolm informed us one day of the following conversation at Longwood. 'Why should I see those people?' said Bonaparte. 'Who sends them? Is it Austria whom I have had twenty times at my feet? Does Baron Stürmer bring me news of my wife, of my son? And the Emperor Alexander, to whom I rendered such services after the peace of Tilsit—what has he done to make my lot any happier in the wretched position where I am today? By seeing the Commissioners, would I not recognize myself a prisoner of Europe? I am yours in fact because you are keeping me, but not by right.' While the ex-Emperor was expressing himself thus he was doing all he could to obligate us to see him as individuals. Montholon and Gourgaud came very often to the city, tried to meet us there, flattered Monsieur de Montchenu. Las Cases informed me through a lady of society that if he should see me walking he would walk in front of me and take me to his master. Little Betsy Balcombe's letters assured me that her friend Bony was quite impatient to talk with me. From several other quarters we received messages, and my colleagues would have been able to prove the presence of Napoleon Bonaparte on St Helena a hundred times a day if they had wished to content themselves with those means. On July 17 Baron Stürmer finally unearthed among his papers the Convention of August 2. On the twentieth he was called to a second conference at the Governor's, the crux of the question still being the manner of seeing the prisoner. Monsieur de Montchenu maintained that he could see him only as a Commissioner, that to act otherwise would be to fail in his mission and to compromise the dignity of his Court. Stürmer was of the same opinion. Sir Hudson Lowe made some very apt remonstrances. He acknowledged that his personal relations with Bonaparte were hardly satisfactory, that he could not make up his mind to humiliate such a remarkable personage, that Lord Bathurst had not given him instructions on this point and predicted that only disagreeable things for everybody could result from their extraordinary representations. Speaking in my turn, I repeated what I had not ceased to say since my arrival, that, it being useless to expect Bonaparte's consent to the measures adopted toward him, I would do without an official interview, that it would suffice for me to meet him informally while walking, that I might be able, without lacking in my respect, to invite myself to his home like Admiral Malcolm and so many English officers, but that I had done nothing or would do nothing to give the impression of following a separate course of action.

M. de Montchenu pointed out to me that, his instructions and those of Baron Stürmer having been drawn up at the conference of Paris, I ought to conform to them. I answered him that I would look out for that, but that to bring in my chief in an affair not only futile, but for which I could see only a bad result, would hardly be worthwhile. The result of this long discussion was that the Austrian and French Commissioners addressed to the Governor an official note, a copy of which is joined to this report. On the twenty-first this note and the Convention of August 2 were sent to Count Montholon. To this Sir Hudson Lowe added a letter and pointed out that if Bonaparte decided to receive my colleagues I should be likewise presented, although not having had any part in this negotiation. On August 27 the reply came from M. de Montholon which has not yet been communicated to us in its entirety. There was inserted therein a very imperfect extract in the three letters enclosed which he addressed to us on this occasion.

The French Commissioner realized today that his inconsiderate zeal, or rather his extreme stupidity, has considerably embarrassed our progress at St Helena. In this respect the Austrian is guiltless. It was strongly recommended him never to be in opposition to the other. To enable your Excellency to judge of the difficulties of these gentlemen, I have copied word for word what M. de Stürmer says of them in his report to Count Metternich. 'The result of the letter from M. de Montholon is that we must either give up trying to see him or have recourse to unpleasant means. The Governor gives us to understand that he would not refuse to lend us assistance if we officially asked it, but here are the words which he used: 'You alone will be responsible for the consequences which this may entail. You know that Bonaparte has said that Napoleon would fire on whoever would force his door. Suppose I put at your disposition a company of soldiers. What would happen? I would not be surprised if someone were killed. It is impossible to foresee to what insults you would unnecessarily expose yourself and hence your Sovereigns. Furthermore, you must consider, gentlemen, whether such an act against the very person of Bonaparte would secure the approbation of your Governments. There is no doubt that all the Powers are in agreement that he should be treated with the greatest respect. What will you risk after all by forgetting about the whole thing and by waiting for new orders from your Court? But whatever you decide, you will find me ready to assist you.' It will not escape your Excellency that our pride may have carried us to extremes and that it has seemed difficult to give up our object of controlling the man whom nobody has ever yet been able to control. However, the fear of rendering still more disagreeable the position of the Governor, the reasons which he gave us which certainly were considerable, and still more our respect for the bonds of relationship which unite Bonaparte to the august Imperial Family, and to serve the houses of Europe, have determined us to halt in this affair until we can receive new instructions.'

My conduct in this affair was generally approved. All realize the high and generous sentiments of our August Master, and Bonaparte himself is satisfied with them. A Frenchman of his suite whom I recently met in the city approached me very politely and said: 'The Emperor knows that you did not sign the note of the Commissioners. He is sensitive to this honest procedure and has charged me to thank you for it.'

I have the honour to be, etc.

P.S. Your Excellency will find herewith an exact copy of the entire letter of Monsieur de Montholon, only an extract of which has the Governor deemed it proper to communicate to us.

Copy of Letter from Lowe to the Russian Commissioner

August 27, 1816.

Though no specific demand was made by you to me founded on the terms of the Convention to procure you the opportunity of an official interview with Napoleon Bonaparte, yet in compliance with your wishes to me I expressed my desire of introducing you to him. I have since received a letter from General Count Montholon and have the honour to send you the following extract therefrom:

Monsieur le Général:

I have received the Convention of August 2, 1815, concluded between His Britannic Majesty, the Emperor of Austria, the Emperor of Russia, and the King of Prussia, which was enclosed in your letter of July 21. . . .

Against the contents of that treaty the Emperor Napoleon protests. Commissioners from Austria and Russia have arrived at St Helena. If the object of their mission is to fulfil a part of the duty which these Emperors have contracted through the treaty of August 2 and to insure the fact that the English agents in a little colony in the midst of the ocean should not fail in the respect to a Prince bound with them by ties of relationship and by so many other connections we recognize in that negotiation traits of character of these two Sovereigns.* They have come here to enforce the terms of the Convention. They have no concern for the care of his person but are here simply to prove his existence. But you have assured us, sir, that these Commissioners had neither the right nor the power to have any opinion on anything which may happen in this island.

* My explanations were when I first mentioned the arrival of the commissioners and mentioned their desire of seeing Napoleon Bonaparte. (Lowe.)

As you had made no application for an official interview with Napoleon Bonaparte, the remarks respecting his Majesty the Emperor of Russia were, of course, wholly uncalled for, but they refer as I conceive more to his signature of the Convention and to your arrival on this island than to any proceeding on your part.

Though the assumption of the title of Emperor by Napoleon Bonaparte as expressed in Count Montholon's letter renders his communication not official, yet as it is the only one that has been received, I did not delay sending the above extract for your information.

I have the honour, etc.
HUDSON LOWE,
LT. GEN.

Copy of a Letter from Count Montholon to Sir Hudson Lowe

Monsieur le Général,

I have received the Convention of August 2, 1815, concluded between his Britannic Majesty, the Emperor of Austria, the Emperor of Russia, and the King of Prussia, enclosed in your letter of July 21 last. The Emperor Napoleon protests against the contents of that treaty.[26] He is in no sense the prisoner of England. After having left his abdication in the hands of the representatives of the nation, in accordance with the constitution adopted by the French people, in favour of his son, he gave himself voluntarily and freely to England in order to live there as a private citizen, in retirement under the protection of the British laws. The violation of all laws cannot constitute a right. As a matter of physical fact, the person of the Emperor Napoleon is in the power of England. But neither in fact nor of right has he been in the power of Austria, Russia, Prussia, even according to the laws of England, which has never concerned itself with the prisoners of the Russians, the Austrians, the Prussians, the Spaniards, the Portuguese, although united to these Powers by treaties of alliance and making war conjointly with them. The Convention of August 2, made two weeks after Napoleon's arrival in England, can have no effect in law; it offers the spectacle of the combination of four of the greatest Powers of Europe for the oppression of one man, a combination disavowed by the opinion of all the peoples of those Powers, as well as by all the principles of reason and moral sanity. The Emperors of Austria and of Russia and the King of Prussia having in fact and of right no control over the person of the Emperor Napoleon, they have not been able to enact any decrees relative to him. If the Emperor Napoleon had been in the power of the Emperor of Austria, that Sovereign would have remembered the bonds with which religion and nature had linked a father and a son, bonds which are never violated with impunity. He would have recalled that four times Napoleon restored him to his throne—at Leoben in 1797 and at Lunéville in 1801, when his armies were under the walls of Vienna, at Presbourg in 1806, and at Vienna in 1809, when his soldiers were masters of the capital and of three fourths of the kingdom. That Sovereign would have remembered the protestations which he made to him at the bivouac of Moravia in 1806 and at the interview of Dresden in 1812.

If the person of the Emperor Napoleon had been in the power of the Emperor Alexander, he would have remembered the bonds of friendship contracted at Tilsit and during twelve years of almost daily intercourse. He would have remembered the conduct of the Emperor Napoleon on the day after the battle of Austerlitz, where, although able to make him a prisoner together with the remnants of his army, he contented himself with the Czar's word, and allowed him to conduct his retreat. He would have remembered the perils which the Emperor Napoleon personally braved to extinguish the flames at Moscow and to preserve for him his capital. Certainly that Sovereign would not have known how to violate the duty imposed by friendship and gratitude toward a friend in adversity.[27]

If the person of the Emperor Napoleon had been in the power of the King of Prussia, that Sovereign would not have forgotten that the Emperor Napoleon, after Friedland, might have placed another Prince on the Prussian throne. He would surely not have forgotten in the face of a disarmed enemy the protestations of devotion and the sentiments which he showed him in 1812 at the interview of Dresden. Accordingly we see, by Articles 2 and 5 of the said treaty, that, not being able to influence in any way the fate of the person of the Emperor Napoleon, which is not in their power, these monarchs trust to whatever dispositions his Britannic Majesty may make, and he will be charged with fulfilling all obligations.

These monarchs have reproached the Emperor Napoleon for having preferred the protection of British law to theirs. The false ideas which the Emperor Napoleon had of the liberality of English laws, and of the influence of a great, generous, and free people on its government, persuaded him to prefer the protection of its laws to those of his father-in-law or his old friend the Emperor of Russia. The Emperor Napoleon always had the power of assuring what was personal to him by a diplomatic treaty, by putting himself at the head of either the Army of the Loire, or of the Army of the Gironde commanded by General Clausel.[28] But, seeking henceforth only retirement and the protection of the laws of a free nation, either England or America, any stipulation appeared useless to him. He believed the English people bound more stringently by its frankness and nobility than it would have been by the most solemn treaties. But that error will forever make true Britons blush; and in the present generation, as in future generations, it will be a proof of the disloyalty of the English administration.

[All these reasonings are superfluous. But it is thus that Bonaparte judges and will always judge his position. He will protest up to his last breath against the Convention of August 2. 'The Emperor,' Gourgaud recently said to me, 'never acknowledged himself anybody's prisoner. Never will he receive the Commissioners of the Allied Powers. If those from Austria and France want to force his doors, he will have himself killed before allowing it.'—Balmain.]

Austrian and Russian Commissioners have arrived at St Helena. If the object of their mission is to fulfil a part of the duty which the Emperors of Austria and Russia have contracted by the treaty of August 2 and to see that the English agents in a little colony in the middle of the ocean should not fail to show proper respect to a Prince bound to them by ties of relationship and so many other connections, it would be in keeping with the characters of these two Sovereigns. But, sir, you have given assurances that these two Commissioners had neither the right nor the power to hold any opinion on anything which can happen on this rock.

The English Ministry has had the Emperor Napoleon transported to St Helena, two thousand leagues from Europe. This rock, situated in the tropics, five hundred leagues from any continent, is a prey to the devouring heat of this latitude, and for three quarters of the year is covered with clouds and fogs. It is at once the driest and dampest country in the world. This climate is most disturbing to the Emperor's health. [It is a fact that there are many sick people an St Helena.[29] Inflammatory fevers are making terrible ravages this year, especially in the garrison. The Sixty-sixth Infantry has lost a quarter of its number. Gourgaud feared he would die of dysentery, from which Montholon also suffered. But Bonaparte is well, and this climate does not disturb his health. If he occasionally has slight indispositions it is because he eats too much and gets no exercise.—Balmain.]

It is hatred which inspired the choice of this spot and the instructions given by the Ministry to the English officers commanding the country. They were ordered to call the Emperor Napoleon 'General,' wishing to make him acknowledge that he never reigned in France. That decided him not to take an incognito name, as he had contemplated doing on leaving France. First Magistrate of the Republic for life, under the title of First Consul, he signed the Preliminaries of London and the Peace of Amiens with the King of Great Britain. He received as Ambassadors Lord Cornwallis, Messrs. Merry and Cathcart, who in that capacity spent some time at his Court. He accredited to the King of England Count Otto and General Andréossy, who as Ambassadors resided at the Court of Windsor. When, after an exchange of letters between the Ministries of Foreign Affairs of the two monarchies, Lord Lauderdale came to Paris furnished with full powers from the King of England, he treated with the plenipotentiaries of the Emperor Napoleon and stayed some months at the Court of the Tuileries. When, since then, Lord Castlereagh signed at Châtillon the ultimatum which the Allied Powers presented to the plenipotentiaries of the Emperor Napoleon, by that fact they collectively acknowledged his dynasty. This ultimatum was more advantageous than the Treaty of Paris, but it required that France give up Belgium and the left bank of the Rhine, which was contrary to the propositions of Frankfort and the proclamations of the Allied Powers, which was contrary also to the oath by which at his coronation the Emperor Napoleon had pledged the integrity of his Empire. At that time the Emperor considered that the natural limits of France were a guaranty as well of the equilibrium of Europe.

The treaty of August 2 and the Act of Parliament call the Emperor Napoleon by the name of Bonaparte and do not give him the title of General. Without doubt the title of General Bonaparte is eminently glorious. The Emperor bore it at Lodi, at Castiglione, at Rivoli, at Arcola, at Leoben, at the Pyramids, at Aboukir. But for seventeen years he has borne that of First Consul and Emperor. To allow that contention would be to agree that he never was both First Magistrate of the Republic and Sovereign of the Fourth Dynasty. It is the English Parliament itself which has changed more than once the reigning dynasty owing to changes in popular opinion; kings are but hereditary magistrates who exist for the good of their nations—not nations for the happiness of their kings.

[This digression is but verbiage. The Government called him General because it could not do otherwise. If it had said simply Bonaparte, or Napoleon Bonaparte, it would have been taxed with incivility; and to say

Napoleon the Great, or not to name him at all, is impossible. So they are forced to call him General, and he has erred in not taking an incognito name.—Balmain.]

It is the same spirit of hatred which inspired the order that the Emperor Napoleon should not write or receive any letter which has not been opened and read by the English Ministry and the officers of St Helena.

Through that order it is impossible for him to receive news of his mother, his wife, his son, and his brothers. And, when desiring to prevent the embarrassment of seeing his letters read by subaltern officers, he wished to send sealed letters to the Prince Regent, the answer was that only opened letters might pass, that such were the orders of the Ministry. Letters arrived for the officers of the Emperor's suite; they were unsealed and were handed to you, but you did not forward them because they had not been inspected by the English Ministry. They had to be sent back again four thousand leagues, and the officers in question had the pain of knowing that news from their families was close at hand but that they could not be acquainted with it for another six months. One's heart revolts at it.

[All this happened before our arrival and is not easy to verify, for the English deny these assertions and the French repeat them. But it is certain that all the Longwood correspondence is opened either by the English Ministry or the Governor of St Helena. As for newspapers, Bonaparte receives as many as arrive. Never have European affairs been concealed from him.—Balmain.]

We have not been able to subscribe to the *Morning Chronicle*, to the *Morning Post*, or to any French papers. From time to time a few copies of the *Times* have been sent over to Longwood. Pursuant to a request made on board the *Northumberland*, some books have been sent, but all those dealing with affairs of recent years have been carefully excluded. An English author who had made a trip through France and had then published in London a book about his travels wanted to send the Emperor a copy. But you did not allow him to have it because the gift did not have your Government's approval. It is said that the other books have been kept back because they were inscribed either to the Emperor Napoleon or to Napoleon the Great. The English Ministry is not authorized to impose any of these vexations. The Act of Parliament, iniquitous as it is, considers the Emperor Napoleon as a prisoner of war. But never have prisoners of war been forbidden to receive newspapers or books. Such orders go back to the days of the Inquisition.

All communication with St Helena by the sea is impossible. There is only one little city, Jamestown, where vessels can anchor.

[The interior of the island is not forbidden to Bonaparte, nor is the town. He never goes out of his enclosure because he does not like to see the sentries, nor is he willing to be accompanied by an English officer, Even from Longwood a horseback ride may be made of eight to ten miles. It is a spacious, open terrain and the only spot on the island where one can gallop.—Balmain.]

The Emperor has been established in a place called Longwood, exposed to every wind, a barren spot, uninhabited, without water or verdure. [This passage from Count Montholon's letter is absolutely true. Plantation House is a magnificent place, well situated, with gardens and fountains; and Longwood is only a hovel, surrounded with gum-trees (a dreadful tree which gives no shade), and very windy.[30] In general, the English treat Bonaparte very shabbily. His house, his people, his dress, all are mean. He has only the necessities. That enormous expense which so excited Parliament is wholly for the maintenance of the troops and guard-ships, and of a numerous and more or less useless staff.—Balmain.] There is an enclosure of about 1,200 square toises[31] where a camp has been established. Admiral Malcolm had his sailors put up a tent in the only shady spot.

Longwood was originally constructed as a grange for the company's farm, and then served as country house for the Vice-Governor, who had some bedrooms added. For over a year workmen have been inside, and the Emperor has had the inconvenience of living in a house under construction. His bedroom is too small to hold a bed of ordinary size, but every change at Longwood would prolong the carpenters' stay. And yet on this wretched island there are lovely sites, offering fine trees, gardens, and rather pretty houses, among which is Plantation House. But the positive instructions of the Ministry forbid you to suggest this house, which would have spared your treasury much expense.

You have forbidden all communication between us and the inhabitants of the island. [This is also true. Since the departure of Admiral Cockburn, Sir Hudson Lowe has increased the means of surveillance in an incredible manner, and there is no extravagance of which he is not capable to assure himself of the safety of his prisoner.—Balmain.] You have, in fact, held Longwood *incomunicado*. You seem, then, to have taken particular pains to deprive us of all the slight resources and comforts which this wretched island offers, and we are not otherwise than if we were on the barren rock of Ascension Island. During the four months that you have been here the Emperor's position has grown steadily worse. Count Bertrand pointed out to you that you were even violating the laws of your own Parliament, that you were trampling on the rights of prisoners of war. You answered that you recognized only the letter of your instructions and that they were even stricter than your conduct appeared to us.

I have the honour to be, etc.

P.S. I had signed this letter before receiving yours of the seventeenth. You enclose the account for a new amount of 20,000 pounds sterling which you judge necessary for the expenses of Longwood after having made all the reductions which you thought possible. The discussion of this account cannot concern us in any manner. The Emperor's table is already reduced to bare necessities. [He has ordinary daily fare, and a rather bad cook. As for provisions, there is no storehouse on this rock, and the English Government is not willing to go to the expense of four or five transports to establish regular communication with the Cape, the African coast, or Brazil; it is, then, impossible to have any of good quality.—Balmain.] All the provisions are of bad quality and four times dearer than at Paris. You ask for 12,000 pounds sterling for the Emperor, your Government allowing you only 8,000 pounds sterling for all his expenses. I have had the honour to say to you that the Emperor has no money, that for a year he had received no letter, and that he was completely ignorant of what was happening or might happen in Europe. The Emperor has always desired and still desires to provide for all his needs, and he will do so as soon as you shall make it possible for him, by ceasing to forbid the tradesmen of the island to serve him by means of correspondence and as soon as such letters will no longer be submitted to examination. As soon as his needs are known in Europe, those persons who are interested in him will send him the necessary funds. [Although this letter was shown me confidentially, I believed it my duty, on account of this striking passage, to communicate it to the Austrian and French Commissioners.—Balmain.]

Lord Bathurst's letter which you communicated to me causes strange emotions. [This letter must be that in which Lord Bathurst recommends to Sir Hudson Lowe to make public at Longwood the Act of Parliament. See my report No. 8.—Balmain.) Are your Ministers not aware that the spectacle of a great man at grips with adversity is the most sublime spectacle? Are they unaware that Napoleon at St Helena, in the midst of persecutions of all kinds—to which he opposes only serenity—is greater, more revered, than on the most powerful throne in the world, where for so long he was the arbiter of kings? Those who show no respect to Napoleon in his present position demean their own characters and the nation which they represent.

* * *

In communication No. 7, dated 10 October 1816, Count Balmain protests against the refusal of his request for an increased allowance, saying that it is absolutely impossible for him to live on the island on anything less than 2,200 pounds sterling annually. If the Government persists in its refusal, the Commissioner will have no choice but to send in his resignation, the alternative being ruinous indebtedness. 'By the time any new decision can reach me, I shall have been here for eighteen months. Neither my health nor my private affairs will allow me to go on for longer than two years.' In any case, he is of the opinion that by that time the maintenance of Commissioners will become unnecessary, for public opinion in Europe will then have become much less interested in the whole matter of the exile.

* * *

No. 8

October 10, 1816.

I have the honour to transmit herewith the copy of a letter and two enclosures which the Governor of St Helena has just addressed to me, to which I have as yet made no reply. The Austrian and French Commissioners received the same communication. M. de Montchenu has entered into explanations with Sir Hudson Lowe, and when they have settled the affair I shall not fail to give your Excellency a report. In the meantime I beg you to enlighten me on my procedure.

Admiral Malcolm has left St Helena to visit the Cape of Good Hope station. His absence will not be long, and we hope to see him again in two months.

I have the honour to be, etc.

Plantation House,
October 9, 1816.

The Governor presents his respects to Count Balmain, and has the honour to communicate for his information that in the despatches he has received by the last arrivals from England, he is instructed to have it understood by all persons living at St Helena, or resorting to it, that they are considered to be so far owing allegiance to his Britannic Majesty as to come within the provisions of the Act of Parliament which has been promulgated here for the safe custody of Napoleon Bonaparte. He begs leave to enclose extracts from the only letters which he has received on this subject, one which is of a general nature, and the other regarding the persons who followed Napoleon Bonaparte to this island.

Extract of a letter from Earl Bathurst, dated Downing Street, July 17, 1816

As you make the Act of Parliament known, you must take care to have understood that all persons living at St Helena, or resorting to it, are considered as so far owing allegiance to his Majesty as to come within the provisions of the act.

True extract.
H. Lowe.

Extract of a letter from Earl Bathurst, dated Downing Street, July 9, 1816 Respecting the Persons Who Followed General Bonaparte to the Island of St Helena

Previous to your requiring their signature to the paper (i.e., that in which their consent is to be expressed for remaining in the island of St Helena), you should explain to them that whilst remaining at St Helena they would be subject to the provisions of the Act of Parliament, 56 George III, cap. 22, by which all persons (who are subjects of his Majesty or owing allegiance to him, and *which allegiance they do owe whilst they are permitted to reside in his dominions*) assisting in or privy to the escape of General Bonaparte are considered guilty of felony.

No. 9

December 1, 1816.

No sooner was Count Montholon's letter (annexed to my report No. 6) forwarded to Sir Hudson Lowe, than Bonaparte seemed to repent of his decision toward us. He became gloomy, pensive, and for several days fell into a wretched temper. It was not that he considered the possibility of receiving us as Commissioners (on that point his decision is irrevocable), for never will he recognize himself the prisoner of any Power. But he regretted not seeing us at all. An enemy of the English, tired of his solitude, often overcome with ennui, he had need of us to break the monotony of his existence. He realized, moreover, that a more moderate response on his part would sooner or later have arranged the affair to his entire satisfaction, and he blamed himself for having terminated it brusquely, in such a way as to render difficult a reopening of the matter.

On the other hand, having constrained the Governor, the Commissioners of the Allied Powers, and everybody to defer to his will, he has become quite complacent, and soon arrived at a new idea. This was to prevent access to the Longwood enclosure to anyone coming with a permit from the English authorities. He wanted Marshal Bertrand to be the only one to give such permits. Since nothing was more contrary to the regulations of surveillance, this idea was strongly opposed. Piqued to the quick at the refusal, he requested Sir Hudson Lowe never to introduce any strangers to him, and said that in future he would see no one. To this last the Governor, who for a long time had been thinking of isolating his prisoner, gladly consented. Since then people have ceased to go to Longwood. Travellers do not dare even to approach it. Those of the military men and natives of the island who used to be seen there have retired, and that corner of the island, formerly so frequented, is today deserted, and complete silence reigns there.

Bonaparte continues to enjoy perfect health. He is becoming stouter, and has an excellent appetite; he refuses to take any exercise, but nothing hitherto has affected his strong constitution. From time to time rumours of his sickness are circulated. There is a general disturbance at Longwood. The next day we learn that it was only an indigestion or a toothache.

Admiral Malcolm returned on November 28 from his trip to the Cape of Good Hope.

I have the honour to be, etc.

The Departure of Las Cases

The 'happy' family at Longwood stayed intact for only a little over a year. Las Cases was the first to allow his unhappiness and homesickness to take precedence over his pleasure in basking in the shadow of the great. His relations with his fellow-exiles were becoming worse; his health was beginning to give him some trouble; and, assigned to the most uncomfortable rooms at Longwood, he and his son, a lad of sixteen whose health was no better, had become thoroughly miserable. The last straw was added by the Governor's removal of his mulatto servant James Scott. Scott had been detected in the act of sending secret messages to Baroness Stürmer.

Balmain describes correctly the use to which Las Cases hoped to put Scott. The Count was reckless in this intrigue because he did not fear detection, knowing that such a result would bring about his departure from the island without incurring the animosity of Napoleon.

Twice Scott passed through the guard at Longwood; and although it is a purely academic question, his success in doing so gives ground to the supposition, which is discussed in connection with a later episode, that if a mulatto unaided could elude the sentries' vigilance, a clever man like Napoleon, helped by many, could easily have done so.

No. 10

December 8, 1816.

The Counts de las Cases, of Bonaparte's suite, were arrested on November 25 by order of the Governor: the father for having attempted, by bribing an inhabitant of the island, to send letters to Europe, and the son for having aided in the attempt. Sir Hudson Lowe, who is becoming more reticent toward the Commissioners, has told us nothing of the background of the affair. The following details I owe to a well-informed person. Count de las Cases on arriving at St Helena engaged a servant, a very intelligent mulatto named Scott. He soon learned to rely on his faithfulness, and, to put it to the test, charged him with an insignificant but secret message. The Governor was immediately informed of it by the person to whom the message was addressed, and the mulatto was ordered to leave his master. M. de las Cases, with his views as to the usefulness of the man, showed him great kindness, and in order that the latter might have a plausible pretext for reappearing at Longwood, he engaged him to take there a part of his clothes.

The plot now moved rapidly. The Count made up a large volume of letters, and had his son transcribe them in tiny writing on several handkerchiefs of white silk. When this was done, they sewed the handkerchiefs into a waistcoat, and impatiently awaited the mulatto. Two months elapsed before he came. They proposed to him to go to England on the first boat. As he was free, and hoped for a large reward, he did not hesitate. He then put on the waistcoat containing the precious letters, which the mulatto promised on his arrival to hand to a lady named Clavering, who is French by parentage and the widow of an Englishman formerly a prisoner in Antwerp.

Scott, although glad to serve his former masters, was by no means sure of his part. Played upon now by the hope of a happy issue, and now by the fear of a terrible punishment, in order to reassure himself he told all to his father, one of the farmers of the island. The latter wanted to force his son to confess immediately to the Governor, and on the young man's refusal, he tore the fatal waistcoat from him, perceived the handkerchiefs, and carried the whole thing to Plantation House. The son was promptly placed in a cell, and has already undergone several examinations. The Las Cases were arrested the next day.

It is said that Bonaparte has had no hand in this affair and that nothing points to an attempt at escape. However that may be, it is certain that the Governor will never allow the Commissioners to see the handkerchiefs, and that the result will be the same as with Count Montholon's note—we shall have them unknown to him.

Captain Piontkowski and four French domestics at Longwood left on August 19 for the Cape of Good Hope. Sir Hudson Lowe assured me that he had no complaint to make of them and was sending them away solely for reasons of economy.[32]

Bonaparte appears indifferent to all these blows. He did not even ask to see Piontkowski on the day of his departure, and when he learned of the Las Cases adventure, he simply shrugged his shoulders and said, 'He is crazy.'

I have the honour to be, etc.

No. 11

December 24, 1816.

The result of the enquiry into the Las Cases affair has been sent to Lord Bathurst, and until instructions are received father and son will be kept under surveillance. The elder has shown a desire to settle in England. Having lost caste in the Emperor's mind, he says he no longer cares to stay at St Helena. I believe that the affair is of little importance and there was no question of escape.

Among the papers was found a fragment of Bonaparte's history, which was immediately returned to him. His first impulse was to burn it, but the Governor hastened to assure him, on his word of honour, that neither he nor anyone else had any knowledge of it.

Bonaparte remains very melancholy. The loss of Las Cases is a blow to his pride. He affects an indifferent air, but in the depths of his soul there is real suffering. He has been heard to say, 'Let death came now,' and also: 'Let them send back all my French people. I don't want any more with me, so they might just as well send them off under some bad pretext.'

I do not yet go to Longwood and can only judge of Bonaparte's position by what it suits the English to tell me of it. What I am sure of is that he is unhappy and that he has said more than once: 'If I were in the power of the Emperor Alexander I should be better off. That Prince is noble and generous. I should forget my misfortunes.' It is easily to be seen, also, that the Frenchmen of his suite are seeking eagerly to interest everybody in his fate. One day young Las Cases accosted me at the door of my house, to complain bitterly of the English authorities. He told me that the Emperor was badly lodged, badly served, badly fed, that the Governor took offence at everything, that his surveillance was tyrannical. Another day Piontkowski, with an officer of the Fifty-third Infantry, came to my house, although we did not know each other. At first he chatted to me about his squadron of red lancers, which now forms part of the Polish army. Then, suddenly changing his tone, he said, in the presence of the Englishman: 'They are treating us vilely. The Emperor is most unhappy.' At that point I interrupted him and took my leave.

These reports are surely exaggerated. Animosity against the English underlies them all. Yet perhaps they are not entirely wrong. I cannot make up my mind absolutely until we have seen Bonaparte, and it is to be hoped that his door will not forever be closed to the Commissioners.

A short time before his departure for the Cape of Good Hope, Sir Pulteney Malcolm had an interview at Longwood regarding Russia. 'That country,' said Bonaparte, 'will, unless you look out, lay down the law to everybody. She is today strong enough to undertake anything. Her Sovereign is peaceful. That is fortunate, for if he were not, anything might happen. His flying corps, the Cossacks from all over Russia, would overrun Europe.'

Admiral Malcolm asked him what he thought of the Russian soldier. 'He is brave, robust, and patient,' answered Bonaparte.

'But,' said the Admiral, 'it would seem that the Cossacks are not good cavalry.'

'Do not think so,' replied Bonaparte. 'They are intelligent, and more dangerous than you believe. You simply can't get at them, they are so skilful in surprising the enemy, in attacking and then in retiring. They go from one country to another without knowing the language or the roads. They are everywhere, they live on almost nothing, and never have I captured any Cossacks.'

Admiral Malcolm wanted to ask questions regarding the campaign of Moscow, but as usual the other avoided the subject. They then passed to the Russian navy. 'That country,' said Bonaparte, 'has only her coasts to protect. All she needs is a Baltic squadron, which need not be very strong, and another against Turkey. She should not try a naval offensive, for she is not a maritime power.'

I have the honour to be, etc.

P.S. Last night, the twenty-fifth, the Counts de las Cases, to the great surprise of every one, were transferred from the house where they were kept under watch to the Governor's house at St James, where the surveillance is much less strict. It is said that they are soon to leave for England. Las Cases must have said positively that he wishes to see no more of Longwood, and that, determined to leave Bonaparte forever, he desired to live at peace under the protection of the English laws. About this fact Sir Hudson Lowe has communicated to us nothing. M. de las Cases carries away with him precious materials for history. It is quite clear now that that was his aim in coming to St Helena.[33]

No. 12

December 29, 1816.

Sir Hudson Lowe has just informed us that the Counts de las Cases will leave tomorrow by the brig *Griffon* and be taken to the Cape of Good Hope, whence they will probably go to England.

The affair is shrouded in mystery. Some say that the famous handkerchief affair is only a ruse of his own invention to get himself arrested and to leave Bonaparte while appearing to yield to force. Others believe that the project was a serious one, but that, since it did not succeed, Las Cases had the good sense not to return to Longwood, and thus escaped an insupportable exile. Admiral Malcolm leans to the former view. The Governor is still determined to keep us out of the secret. M. de Montchenu pointed out to him, in my hearing, that it was important for the King to see this correspondence on account of the Frenchmen who might be named. 'At London,' Sir Hudson Lowe answered dryly, 'they may perhaps explain the matter to your ambassador.'

This gives your Excellency an idea of our position.

I have the honour to be, etc.

THE YEAR 1817

No. 1

January 6, 1817.

The Austrian Commissioner and the Governor of St Helena are at open war. For about six weeks there has been between them such a continual exchange of notes and explanations as to lead to a probable outburst. The whole of it is concerned with an insignificant object.

A woman named Marchand, attached to the household of the Archduchess Marie Louise and the mother of a *valet de chambre* of Bonaparte, was aware at Vienna that an Austrian botanist named Welle was to follow Baron Stürmer to St Helena. Wishing to profit by that opportunity to send her son a lock of her hair,' she begged M. Boze, head gardener at Schönbrunn, to ask Welle for his good offices, and the latter consented. The hair, which was of a flaxen blond, was enclosed in a packet on which was written: 'I send you some of my hair. If you have any way of getting your portrait made, please send it to me. Your mother, Marchand.'

Shortly after arriving at St Helena Welle came across Marchand in the town and fulfilled his commission, not thinking it necessary to advise Baron Stürmer of it. After a while the rumour began to be circulated that some hair of the King of Rome had arrived in Bonaparte's prison.[35] Soon they said that Welle had brought it from Mme. Marchand, unknown to the English authorities. Enquiries were made at Longwood and everywhere else. Of these the Governor did not communicate to us the result, but they are sure that the message intrusted to Welle is from the King of Rome and that Mme. Marchand simply lent her name. Some draw absurd conclusions against the house of Austria. However that may be, the botanist excited the suspicion of the Governor and his recall was determined.

Baron Stürmer knew nothing of the matter, for they avoided all discussion of it before him. Abruptly Sir Hudson Lowe advised him that Welle, not being provided with special authorization from the British Government to reside at St Helena, and having no doubt purchased during his three months' stay sufficient plants and animals, must now leave the island. The Governor's lack of candour naturally made more out of the affair than it was worth. The Commissioner received the note with bad grace, and thought the Governor's 'officiousness' extremely fantastic. He strongly opposed the expulsion of the botanist. Sir Hudson Lowe made no new move. A correspondence then began between them which was marked by the exchange of three or four official notes a day, in which each treated the other with bitterness and disdain.

It then became apparent that Baron Stürmer knew nothing of the affair previously described. Welle was immediately examined. He declared on oath that he had never either seen or known Mme. Marchand, or suspected that the message with which he was charged could have come from the King of Rome. After this enquiry the Austrian Commissioner tried to come to an understanding with Sir Hudson Lowe. 'You should know,' Lowe said severely, 'that the affair is important, exceedingly important. Letters have been transmitted unknown to me, and it is alleged that you had knowledge of it.'

'Anyone who says that,' cried the other, pale and trembling with anger, 'is a coward and a rascal.' 'What you tell me about Welle,' added the Governor, 'is not enough. I must examine him myself.'

'So you mean to insult me?' cried the Baron. 'No, you will not see Welle. You have no right over him. A Commissioner cannot be treated thus, a man enjoying the confidence of his Sovereign. If the Court of Vienna had desired to send Bonaparte his son's hair, they would have sent it to me, and I would have been more skilful.'

'It is not,' said the Governor, 'that I envy a father the natural pleasure of receiving his child's hair, but they must not make a mystery of it. That is an infraction of the law.'

They spent a whole hour abusing each other. Finally Baron Stürmer enquired if it had been proved that the message in question had not come from Mme. Marchand. Sir Hudson Lowe replied that he would say nothing whatever on that subject. The result of their quarrel was that Welle underwent a second interrogation, in which he simply repeated everything that he had previously stated. Nevertheless the Governor held to his decision, and the Commissioner had to give way.

Welle will leave the island when the pleasant season sets in.[36]

I have the honour to be, etc.

No. 2

January 28, 1817.

The grief which Bonaparte felt at the loss of Las Cases seems to have entirely disappeared. He is gayer than ever, and seems in splendid health, except that he has become a little thinner. It is said that Mme. Montholon has now become his secretary. He continues to receive no one, and hardly ever goes out of his house. Admiral Malcolm, since his return from the Cape, has only seen him twice. The Governor never sees him. Often we are without news of him for three days.

I have the honour to be, etc.

P.S. Your Excellency will permit me to enclose a little sketch of Bonaparte, made in haste at a moment when he was reprimanding Bertrand. It will give an idea of his present costume. As my whole mission here is made up of trifles, I have believed it proper to add this.

No. 3

February 28, 1817.

It is now six months since Bonaparte has seen or received strangers, with the exception of Admiral Malcolm, and nearly three months since he has gone out of the house, even to take the air. He lives alone, without taking any exercise, in a climate where undue repose and solitude easily affect one's health and may cause death. Often, through ennui, he suddenly changes his mode of living. Admiral and Lady Malcolm, who saw him recently, found him somewhat pale and anaemic, but in good humour and extremely affable. While talking of various matters, he pointed out to the Admiral that the Bourbons, who had returned to France on the shoulders of the Allies, would not maintain themselves there, that he alone, of all the heirs of the Revolution, knew how to lead the French people.

'You lead them to victory,' said the Admiral, 'but that is not what makes the public happy nor what they need at this moment.'

'Ah, no,' he replied, 'everything has its limits. I don't want any more war. If I were reigning, I should not lift a finger.' He also said that the Austrians were never liked in Italy; and that the Emperor Francis was a Bluebeard, and that he kills all his women.[37]

The Austrian Commissioner has already borrowed £1000. He had received nearly £3000 from his Government, and these two sums scarcely suffice for his expenses. This proves to your Excellency that nothing is comparable to the dearness of St Helena. I have seen six pounds paid for half of a pig, and sixty are asked for a dozen chairs.

I have the honour to be, etc.

* * *

In his fourth report Count Balmain observes that he has been without news from Europe for five months and accordingly fears that his reports have not been arriving. He sends duplicates of his recent communications.

* * *

No. 5

April 14, 1817.

I take advantage of the departure of one of the Company's vessels to have the honour to send herewith the translation of an edict of the court of Pekin relative to the embassy of Lord Amherst. It is a rather curious document in Chinese diplomacy. The noble lord is expected daily at St Helena. His embassy, as your Excellency will see by this edict, has failed.

Bonaparte continues in good health, and still sees nobody. I shall give news of him at greater length, as soon as possible.

Translation of an Imperial Edict[38]

Dated the fifteenth day of the seventh moon of the twenty-first year (6 September 1816) of Kiu King, addressed to the Keing Kiau, and the Stuysen Tung of Canton, and received the fifth of the eighth moon (25 September).

The English ambassadors, upon their arrival at Tien Sing, have not observed the laws of politeness, in return for the invitation of the Emperor Kiu Chung Tung Chow.[39] Four leagues from the court, they gave us assurances of readiness to perform the prostration and genuflexions required by the laws of good manners of the country, and arrived at the imperial country house, half a league from court, and when we were upon the point of repairing to the hall to receive the embassy, the first as well as the second ambassadors, under pretence of ill health, would not appear; we in consequence passed a decree that they should be sent away upon their return. We, however, reflecting that, although the said ambassadors were blameable, in not observing the laws of politeness toward the sovereign of their country, who from immense distance and over various seas had sent to offer us presents, and to present with respect his letters, indicating a wish to show us due consideration and obedience, contempt was improper and against the maxim to show lenity to our inferiors, in consequence from amongst the presents of the said king we chose the most trifling and insignificant, which are: four maps, two portraits, ninety-five engravings, and, in order to gratify him, accepted them. We in return give as a reward to the said king a yee-yee, a string of rare stones, two pairs of large purses, and four pairs of small purses, and we order the ambassadors to receive these gifts and to return to their kingdom, having so acted in observance of the maxim of Confucius: 'Give much, receive little.'

When the ambassadors received these gifts, they became exceedingly glad and evinced their repentance. They have already quitted Tung Chow. Upon their arrival in Canton, You Kiang and Ting will invite them to an entertainment, in compliance with good manners, and you will make the following speech to them: 'Your good fortune has been small; you arrived at the gates of the imperial house, and were unable to lift your eyes to the face of heaven. The great Emperor reflected that your king sighed after happiness (i.e., China) and acted with sincerity. We therefore accepted some presents, and gifted to your king various precious articles. You must return thanks to the Emperor for his benefits, and return with speed to your kingdom, that your king may feel a respectful gratitude for these acts of kindness; take care to embark the rest of the presents with safety that they may not be lost or destroyed.'

After this lecture, should the ambassador supplicate you to receive the rest of the presents, answer in one word: a decree has passed; we cannot therefore present troublesome petitions, and with decision you will rid yourself of them.

Respect this.

No. 6

May 1, 1817.

Sir Hudson Lowe continues to show us great respect and to extend us his good offices in every way. But our official relations are less satisfactory, and I much doubt, when I recall the daily experience which I have had for ten months, whether the Commissioners and the English authorities will ever be able to get along well together.

In the first place, Bonaparte is the prisoner of Europe. But he is in the power of the English, whom he detests, and of whom he believes he has good reason to complain. From this hostility, which he can show in his immediate environment, there develops in him a need of seeing the Commissioners in order to let loose against the British Government and to interest the other Courts in his favour. This naturally irritates the English and is unfavourable to us, for they hold us responsible in some way for the sorry temper of a man whom everything on this rock should please! 'The fact is,' they say, 'that ever since the arrival of the Commissioners, Longwood has been in insurrection: they have conceived vain hopes there; peace and tranquillity have fled.' Hence in large part results the bad temper that they have shown toward us, which we recognize is through no one's fault.

Secondly, when the Act of Parliament was published at St Helena—i.e., the act specifying the penalty of death for anyone who helped in whatever way to facilitate Bonaparte's escape—the Governor, thinking that we were included, addressed to each of the Commissioners the note and the enclosures, copies of which your Excellency will find enclosed. My French colleague lost no time in starting an argument, and maintained that the act could not concern him, as he was not answerable to any English Court. As Lord Bathurst's letter made no express mention of the Commissioners, the Governor did not believe it necessary to insist on this point. But he now seems to mistrust us and keeps us out of touch with affairs. He takes umbrage at all we do. He has us spied on. When asked why, he replies, 'You are exempted from the law of Parliament, and my position toward you is becoming embarrassing.' 'You reproach me,' he said one day to Baron Stürmer, 'for trusting Admiral Malcolm and not you, but you must realize that I can have him hanged and not you.' The absurdity of this argument is easily apparent, but he sustains it vehemently, becomes violently angry whenever anyone makes the slightest objection.

Thirdly, Sir Hudson Lowe is without any doubt a worthy man, a man of recognized honour and probity. Moreover, he is a cultured man, and they say writes excellently.[40] But in business matters he shows a narrow mind. The responsibility with which he has been charged makes him tremble, and he becomes alarmed at the slightest incident, puzzles his brain for hours over nothing, and does with vast trouble what anyone else would do in a minute. As soon as he is questioned about Bonaparte or anyone in his suite, his forehead becomes wrinkled with suspicion: he believes there is a trap laid for him, and returns only a half-answer. When he explains something to you, he hides its sequel, and never expresses himself logically or clearly, the result being that your mind is hopelessly entangled. Moreover, as I have hinted, he is easy to anger. Let anyone contradict or argue, he knows not what he says or where he is, and he loses his head. To have business with him, and to be comfortable or pleasant with him, are two incompatible things.

Such, Monsieur le Comte, are my official relations at St Helena. We are either disliked, because Bonaparte wants to make his position clear to us, or mistrusted, because we are not subject to English laws. All our discussions and remonstrances on the subject have been of no avail, because the Governor is an intractable man.

Accordingly, our rôle, which was to have been only passive, is altogether negligible. In spite of the deep displeasure which I sometimes feel, I dare to assure your Excellency that my conduct toward the English has always conformed to my instructions. Like my colleagues, I have had long and detailed explanations regarding all these bickerings. I have more than once reproached Sir Hudson Lowe for his mistrust and ill-will toward us, but without becoming angry or pushing him to the limit, and when I saw that I was losing my time and trouble, I left him to the Austrian and French Commissioners, and my conscience is clear.

General Gourgaud, whom I met while walking this morning, assured me that Bonaparte was very impatient to see us. 'He has,' Gourgaud said, 'very friendly feelings for you. Come and see him informally. You will give us all great pleasure.' I thanked him for his frankness, and explained to him briefly that since MM. Stürmer and de Montchenu had not as yet received any reply from Europe regarding the report, I owed it to them not to make any separate move, but that when this matter was disposed of, I should arrange with the Governor regarding the manner of seeing Bonaparte.

That is what I really count on doing as soon as these new orders, which we impatiently await, have arrived.

I have the honour to be, etc.

No. 7

May 6, 1817.

Since Bonaparte has shut himself up within four walls, his life offers no interesting detail. His health is good. He studies, reviews all his campaigns, amuses himself in tracing out the military maps of these battles, and works without relaxation on his history. That is all that we know of him. Admiral Malcolm sees him from time to time, but there is coldness between them. Bonaparte is tired of him, as of all the English. Lately he said to him: 'I made war on Russia only to re-establish the Kingdom of Poland. I should have done better, perhaps, to march on St Petersburg, but I feared to be without provisions there.' It has been noticed that he much prefers his Egyptian campaign.

I have just learned, Monsieur le Comte, that the botanist Welle handed to General Gourgaud, the day after our arrival here and unknown to the English authorities, a letter and a silk handkerchief. As he did not speak of this message to anyone, even when he was questioned at the time of the affair of Mme. Marchand, it is clear that he is under suspicion, and that they did well to send him away.

I have the honour to be, etc.

No. 8

July 4, 1817.

Admiral Malcolm has just been recalled from his post and will set sail today for England. Admiral Plampin, who replaces him, arrived on June 29.[41] For about three months Sir Pulteney Malcolm and the Governor have been at odds. They have ceased to see each other, to invite each other to dinner, or to confer. They say (but the truth of this I do not guarantee) that the former has intrigued at London to supplant the other. The apparent reason for this misunderstanding is that the Admiral greatly underestimated the amount of food necessary at St Helena, that we have lacked wine, flour, and fresh meat, that all the horses on the island, except those at Longwood, are still on half-rations, and that the Governor is the one blamed.

For my part, I can only regret Sir Pulteney Malcolm. On every occasion he has shown me much confidence, and I have always enjoyed his friendship and his advice.

The Austrian and French Commissioners have received orders not to insist on seeing Bonaparte in their official capacities. Monsieur de Stürmer has been severely reprimanded by Prince Metternich on the affair of the lock of hair from the King of Rome, and on his conduct in general. Monsieur de Montchenu has obtained an annual increase of 6000 francs, retroactive to the day of his arrival at St Helena, June 18, 1816.

Lord Amherst, on his return from China, spent some days on the island. Through Marshal Bertrand he solicited an audience at Longwood and was beautifully received. They were an hour together. Bonaparte has an inflammation of the face. His head is swollen, and he has trouble with his teeth. His doctor advises extraction, but he will not hear of the operation and prefers to suffer.

I have the honour to be, etc.

No. 9

July 4, 1817.

The Governor has this moment sent me, the vessel being just about to set sail, the note and enclosure which I have the honour to transmit herewith. I do not yet know what could have caused this proceeding.

I have the honour to be, etc.

[Copy]

The Castle, Jamestown, July 3, 1817.

The Governor presents his respects to Count Balmain and begs to enclose for his information copy of the last reports he has received respecting the state of health of General Bonaparte, who within these few days past has been afflicted with catarrh and appears to be suffering under it.

(Here follow five reports from Dr O'Meara regarding the catarrhal trouble already mentioned.)

No. 10

July 8, 1817.

Recently the Governor invited to his house the Commissioners of the Allied Powers and announced to them (1) that he had received orders to communicate to each of them, separately, everything which had to do with Bonaparte's health. In conformity with these orders, he has sent me the two bulletins from Dr O'Meara which I herewith transmit; (2) that the Prince Regent had excepted them individually from the Act of Parliament, but that in the future their people would be collectively affected. MM. Stürmer and de Montchenu observe with considerable displeasure that the wife of the former and the aide-de-camp of the latter are answerable to the English authorities.

Ever since the arrival of the *Conqueror*, Bonaparte has been eager to see us. He knows that the affair of the trial is over, and that the Austrian and French Commissioners can go to Longwood as private persons. Gourgaud seeks me out and follows me everywhere, pressing me urgently to give pleasure to his master. Bertrand does the same for Mme. Stürmer. The other day, while seated near her, he pretended, in order not to be heard by anyone, to pick up a handkerchief, and whispered: 'Madame, in the name of Heaven, come to see the Emperor. He is expecting you. He speaks only of you. He needs company. He sees only the English, and is very sad.'

Sir Pulteney and Lady Malcolm, before leaving St Helena, made a farewell visit to Bonaparte. He was carried away with invectives against the Prince Regent, Parliament, Ministers, and all the English. Whether it was to keep in his good graces or from timidity, the Admiral listened patiently and said nothing. This silence pleased the great man. He presented Lady Malcolm with a pretty china cup, and assured them of his friendship. The Governor, indignant at this conduct, and because the naval officers chattered about it, immediately proceeded to the Admiral's and made a scene. The latter energetically defended himself, and they wrote their official versions of the affair, which apparently were each sent to Lord Bathurst.

Admiral Plampin is a good man, timid, quite amiable, who wishes to live peacefully and to mix into nothing which does not concern him. He has seen Bonaparte once and made no impression on his mind, for which he is rather glad. To the great scandal of the colony, he brought a lady with him from London, who, though she uses his name, is only his mistress.

I have the honour to be, etc.

(There follow two reports from Dr O'Meara testifying to the complete restoration of Bonaparte's health.)

No. 11

July 20, 1817.

As I had the honour of stating to your Excellency, in my sixth report, that before seeing Bonaparte I was waiting for the replies from Europe regarding the affair of the trial, I went recently to the Governor and unofficially explained to him my intentions. I gave him the following note:

> General:
>
> Since there is now no obstacle to the Commissioners seeing Napoleon as private individuals, I, like your compatriots (notably Lord Amherst), beg to request you to authorize me to make the usual overtures to Count Bertrand. If you would be kind enough to accompany me there I should be doubly grateful.

I had advised him of this move a month previously and at that time found him ready to help me; he even encouraged me. Yet here is the answer he gave me when we came to the point:

> I cannot do it. I have no orders which would authorize it. Write again to your ministers. You see, you are exempted from the law of Parliament. Any Englishman can be hung. Your case is different from ours. On the other hand, Bonaparte treats me outrageously, like a dog. He insults and slanders me. He would say dreadful things to you. I cannot stand it. Since the Commissioners' arrival—I cannot hide it from you—we have been completely at variance. That man is too subtle. He makes plans and dreams visions as if he were still at the Tuileries. I know worthy people (e.g., Malcolm) who, without wishing it or even knowing it, have become his tools. His retinue are all terrible; they are all conspirators. Your position is difficult, painful, extraordinary, I know. So is mine, and you must help me, defend me, make my interests yours.

It would have been easy to refute his logic, but instead of arguing I preferred to retract my request.

I have the honour to be, etc.

P.S. I had finished this report when I received the note from the Governor which I have the honour to enclose. In the margin I have added my memoranda on its contents. It is a detailed and semi-official reply to my little note. He wishes, as is usual with him, to drag out a correspondence, because it is much easier for him to write than to talk. But I have had to tell him that I would not please him in this intention.

Sir:

In reply to your letter, I do myself the honour to inform you that I have not myself received any fresh instruction from Europe on the subject it refers to, nor am I in possession of any definite rule for my guidance, as to the manner in which the Commissioners of the Allied Powers are to be presented to Napoleon Bonaparte. Following only the dictates of my own judgment, after perusal of the convention and of the general instructions under which I act, I am perfectly ready now, as I always have been, to personally introduce you and the other Commissioners to him at any time you may desire, and under any title he may be disposed to receive you, so long as it does not imply a recognition of the pretensions set forth in the reply to the first application I made for your presentation to him.

In respect to authorizing you to visit Count Bertrand, or to conduct you myself to him, for the purpose of being afterward presented by him,[a] I would desire to observe that Count Bertrand holds no official[b] position whatever here, that though through an act of personal consideration toward General Bonaparte he was allowed to accompany him to this island, and from courtesy since has been permitted to introduce private individuals, this can form no just precedent for his introduction of persons in public situation,[c] and I am therefore dispensed from the necessity of considering the application you have addressed to me with respect to him, as of an official nature, while the references it makes to instructions from Europe cannot allow me to regard it wholly as of a private one.[d]

As it is impossible, Sir, however, for you to lay aside the quality of Commissioner, I regret that the application should have been presented, but I am at the same time too solicitous for your favourable judgment and that of the Court you represent, not to enter into a full detail of the reasons which operate against my admission of it.

It is, Sir, in your good recollection that I made known personally to Count Bertrand soon after the arrival of the Commissioners in this island their desire of being presented to Napoleon Bonaparte. I applied afterward by letter through the same person for an opportunity being presented me of introducing them, which letter drew forth a reply full of injurious reflections against my Government and slanderous accusations against myself.

It does not appear, Sir, to me under these circumstances, combined with a view of the relation in which Count Bertrand stands with the present Government of France, suitable to the dignity of the Government I represent, nor to the respect due to my own situation as Governor of this island, to allow him, or any of the French officers who from the indulgence of the British Government were suffered to accompany General Bonaparte here, to be a channel[c] of introduction to or communication between the Commissioners and him; at a time, too, when he has abstracted himself from all personal relation or intercourse with the authorities under which that government has placed him, with the express design perhaps to render himself[f] independent, as far as possible, of their intervention or control.

Your letter, Sir, speaks of the visit to Count Bertrand as a *visite d'usage, à l'exemple de tous vos compatriotes, de Lord Amherst entr'autres.* In pursuance of a regulation established by my predecessor, I have continued to acquiesce in the custom of allowing a previous visit to be made to Count Bertrand by such individuals as were desirous of an opportunity of being admitted to an interview with Napoleon Bonaparte, in order that they might ascertain through him if their visit would be received. The visit to Longwood in such case has never been made without the formality of a pass, signed by myself, valid only for once, and left with the officer of the guard to be returned to me after the visit has been made.

In allowing the continuance of the previous visit to Count Bertrand, I have acted entirely on my own responsibility, for by the instructions of my Government I am particularly cautioned not to suffer previous or after visits to be made to the persons of Genl. Bonaparte's family by those who may have obtained my permission to see *him*. When I have suffered it, therefore, it has solely been from attention to the wishes of Genl. Bonaparte himself, in respect to persons who stood in no official relation[g] towards him, and merely to save him from being importuned by the visits of strangers who might not have obtained his previous consent to their seeing him.

Lord Amherst was here in no official relation that regarded the persons at Longwood. This nobleman from being aware of the delicacy of my own personal relations in that quarter did not make any application to me for being presented until I myself first spoke of it to him.[h] He threw himself entirely upon my[i] judgment in respect to the visit to Count Bertrand, which, time not admitting the possibility of any other[j] arrangement, I did not oppose. Had I thought it could have been considered a ground of precedent upon which to found application for introducing any person in a public situation, I would not however have permitted it.

It is now, Sir, nearly a year since I called on Count Bertrand and personally requested he would make known to Genl. Bonaparte the desire of the lieutenant-colonel and officers of the 66th Regiment to be presented to him at Longwood.[k] To this application no answer was given. I spoke of it afterwards to Genl. Bonaparte himself, in replying to a complaint he made that I had thrown difficulties in the way of the officers seeing him, when he told me that 'the commanding officer ought to have called on the Grand Maréchal himself, and not me.'¹ These officers have not visited Count Bertrand nor seen Genl. Bonaparte. Thus, Sir, you will observe that not *all* my countrymen ('tous vos compatriotes') have had recourse to the intervention of the former. And yet Genl. Bonaparte has latterly intimated that he was ready to receive a visit from these officers. My own visits, and the visits in fact of any person holding authority in the island, as you are well aware, have been very rare.[m] The opposition to a properly regulated intercourse, however, such as my duty would allow me to admit, has rested entirely with him. You will be perhaps surprised when I observe that, from the occasional interviews you had during some of your rides,[n] to which no previous assent was given on my part, you have already conversed more at length with an officer of Genl. Bonaparte's suite than I have done during the whole time of my stay in this island, whilst I am at the same time uninformed of the particulars of any conversation[o] he may have addressed to you, which could not have well occurred with respect to any British subject or official under my own authority.[p]

In thus referring to a past circumstance, I have not, Sir, the presumption to imply a reproach. You are responsible only to the authority from whom your instructions are received. I have spoken of it therefore only to more distinctly point out there has not been that analogy between your situation, even as a private individual, and that of other persons on this island, which the reference to them in your letter 'à l'exemple de tous vos compatriotes' might infer.

In entering into these details I have been, Sir, more solicitous to account for my line of proceeding during the past than to prescribe for the future. Circumstances which have occurred since I received your letter render it very questionable whether I can continue to Count Bertrand that consideration he has hitherto enjoyed. The pretensions invariably manifested through that person require at all times to be strongly[q] repressed. Under no circumstances therefore, particularly at the present moment, could I acquiesce in your desire of being presented to Napoleon Bonaparte through him, unless I rendered myself a voluntary instrument to weaken the force of that authority in which the British Government has placed me, and second the pretensions of those who stand the most opposed,[r] to it, and I am well persuaded I need no other argument, Sir, to induce you to give me the fullest support, in not further pressing your application.[s]

I have the honour to be, etc.

Count Balmain's Marginal Notes

a) This *by him* was not in my note, and entirely changes its purport. I ask to make the customary visit to Count Bertrand. But I beg the Governor to accompany me there, and leave entirely to him the care of arranging the affair. I desire only one thing; that is to be announced as Lieutenant-Colonel Count Balmain, and not as Commissioner from Russia. The rest is indifferent to me. If I neglected to state that precisely, it is because I have explained it to him previously, more than once, and that my application is not official.

b) This observation is out of place. I have said so to him myself a hundred times, and every one at St Helena knows my thought on the subject. Recently, when Gourgaud suggested that I pay a visit to Bertrand, I replied that 'it was not possible to see the "Grand Marshal," since there is no court at Longwood. But whenever possible I should with great pleasure see Count Bertrand, the friend of Napoleon.'

c) The Governor was presented at Longwood by Admiral Cockburn, Admiral Malcolm by the Governor, and so on, each by his predecessor or by his chief. But it is Count Bertrand who announced and introduced all these gentlemen to Bonaparte. None of them could have avoided Bertrand as an intermediary, and I wanted to do the same. The thing seemed to me so natural.

d) This has to do with the orders received by the Austrian and French Commissioners not to insist on seeing Bonaparte personally, but to content themselves with informal means of satisfying themselves of his existence. On account of that, he believes himself obliged to write me a semi-official letter. I do not see the reason of it.

e) Despite this fine reasoning, it was to Montholon that he addressed the note of the Commissioners relative to the trial. So, then, he has recognized someone near Bonaparte; and himself, in a serious and highly official affair, chose that channel of introduction or communication of which he speaks. 'MM. Stürmer and Montchenu,' he said to me then, 'want me to exhibit that man to the people like a bear on a chain. I tell you that I, I who am speaking to you, have not been able to see him in my capacity of Governor.'

f) He does not make a single movement which is not spied upon. He does not say a word which is not reported. He rarely goes out of his house and never out of his enclosure. He writes to no one. He is surrounded with guards, cannon, and ditches. How, then, could he make himself independent? You can reproach him for detesting the Governor. But that does not prevent any of the English, even the officials, from going to Longwood. From the highest officers down to the humblest inhabitant of the island, everybody has been there. Only the Commissioners of the Allied Powers have been excluded, and that is most humiliating.

g) I affirm in all good faith that I did not believe I had any official relation toward a prisoner. Furthermore, I wanted to be presented at Longwood like Admiral Malcolm, a number of generals and officers, the Governor himself; and it was my right.

h) The day following his arrival at St Helena Lord Amherst went to Count Bertrand. Bonaparte had his door refused to him under pretext of indisposition, and the same day received a captain of the India Company. Two days afterward he asked to see his Lordship and gave him a most friendly welcome.

i) I have also trusted to his discretion.

j) Any other arrangement is unheard of up to now. It is a false allegation.

k) Always it is to Count Bertrand that he addresses himself.

l) Despite his explanation at Longwood, he found means, through Bertrand, to arrange this affair. A day was fixed for the officers of the Sixty-sixth Regiment. But those of the *Newcastle* having arrived at the same hour, his were sent back and the navy entered. It was thus that the Sixty-sixth saw neither Bertrand nor Bonaparte. I have this from an eye-witness.

m) His own visits are rare because they are not desired. But Admiral Malcolm made them whenever he felt inclined.

n) Here is the fact. I go out one day on horseback and near Longwood meet General Gourgaud. He offers to go with me, and we spend twenty minutes together talking of this and that. This is the only time since my arrival that I have seen him without company. The next day Admiral Malcolm secretly warns me that the Governor, disturbed at this tête-à-tête, wished to have further information. Not having failed in my duty in any manner, I am quite willing to face him. But he changes his mind and does not trouble me. A few days afterward I meet General Gourgaud again. I pretend not to see him and take another road. He joins me at a gallop. I stop a moment to greet him and answer his civilities. Then I leave him rather quickly. The Governor, alarmed at these two meetings, finally decides to speak to me about them. I tell him of the occurrences as they happened. He thanks me for my frankness, apologizes for having dared to importune me, and even starts in his effusion and embarrassment to tell me of the Las Cases affair. But then he suddenly breaks off and disappears. The affair remains thus.

o) Since Gourgaud spoke to me only of trifles, I did not believe it necessary to render an account of it to the English authorities. If he had made some important disclosure to me I should long hence have written of it to the Imperial Minister.

p) That is false. I know many Englishmen who see Gourgaud and Bertrand, talk for hours with them, and give no account to anyone of what was said. Two officers of high rank, whom I asked about this regulation, have assured me that it never existed.

q) Since that terrible threat, four English officers of my acquaintance have paid the visit to Bertrand.

r) Can it be that St Helena is thus spoken of, in the middle of the ocean, two thousand leagues from Europe, with a garrison of 3000 men and 500 pieces of artillery, and sentries on all sides between Longwood and the sea?

s) Since there is such misunderstanding in this affair, I might have done it all over again in a different way and so have succeeded. But after having reflected on it at great length, I thought it better to give it up and renounce the idea of seeing Bonaparte, and thus not risk imperilling the success of my mission. Accordingly I have made no objection and have not replied to this letter. The Governor is satisfied, and our personal relations are very friendly.

No. 12

July 23, 1817.

I must inform your Excellency that since my last explanation with the Governor I have had another meeting with General Gourgaud near Longwood. As I was not alone, being accompanied by General Bingham, nothing this time constrained me to retire, and I continued my walk together with both these gentlemen.

Gourgaud spoke to me of my visit to Bertrand. 'Since the *Conqueror* has arrived,' he said, 'can we hope to see the Commissioners?'

I told him simply that I had written to the Governor, as was the custom, but that there seemed to be difficulties, and I had to submit to his decision.

'What,' he said, 'not even a little *bonjour* to Mme. Bertrand?'

'Not,' I replied, 'while Longwood and Plantation House are at war. As long as the door of Longwood is closed to Sir Hudson Lowe, not even a little *bonjour* to Mme. Bertrand. Make your peace with him. He is a good man. He means well; he wants to get along with you. You will be asked to his dinners, they will go to see you occasionally, and the time will not seem so long.'

'Ah, sir,' said Gourgaud, 'he made a wrong start. The evil is now without remedy.'

The interview then ended. I am sending this account of it because the circumstance is rather delicate and the Governor attaches importance to the slightest detail.

I have the honour to be, etc.

No. 13, July 26, 1817, transmits a copy of a bulletin of Dr O'Meara on Napoleon's health.

No. 14

August 8, 1817.

Having advised the Imperial Minister in my report No. 7, 1816, that it is impossible to live on St Helena on less than 2200 pounds sterling per year, I cannot fail to inform your Excellency that, after fourteen months' residence in this miserable country, I am in debt to the amount of one thousand pounds from last year. On my conscience I protest that I have lived in an entire lack of luxury. At St James, Longwood, and elsewhere, I have even been criticized for my mode of living, which so little befits the Commissioner of a great Power. In order to give the Minister a new and unanswerable proof of the cost of living here, I have enclosed herewith a certificate from Sir Hudson Lowe regarding Baron Stürmer's expenses. I dare to hope from the justice and kindness of the Emperor that his decision toward my remuneration will be favourable. If it were otherwise, being unable to secure advances on my fortune, I shall be reduced to the tender mercies of my creditors.

I have the honour to be, etc.

Copy of a letter from Sir Hudson Lowe to Baron von Stürmer

November 22, 1816.

I shall draw up with much pleasure the certificate regarding your accounts, and in view of the conversation which we had yesterday, I have no hesitation in declaring to you that the price of all sorts of provisions in this island is at least double what they cost in England; that wine is almost the same price, and in view of our taxes, that makes it quite expensive; that the wages of servants, workmen of all kinds, and field labourers, are at least double and often triple, and the prices of transportation, even for the simplest family needs when one lives in the country, are expensive.*

I shall be glad to draw up an official certificate to this effect.

* Four oxen are harnessed to a wagon to draw barley or oats, and each trip costs eleven Spanish piasters. My moving cost me sixty. —Balmain.

* * *

The reports numbered 15, 16, 18, and 19 transmit bulletins from Dr O'Meara.

No. 17

September 10, 1817.

Since the Governor has taken from me all hope of going to Longwood—his mind being now free from fear in that respect—he is gayer and more affable than has been his custom. It is not so hard now to make him talk, and yesterday we had a long conversation about his last note. What he told me deserves to be faithfully reported to your Excellency.

'Was it Bertrand,' I asked, 'who announced you to Bonaparte when you arrived?'

'Oh, no, it wasn't he. But the fact is I don't really remember. I met him by chance at the door, and he announced me.'

'Well, you see that the thing has happened.'

The Governor, with vehemence: 'I don't approve that arrangement. But Admiral Cockburn having allowed it, I forced myself to allow it too. Bertrand gives himself great airs, which we must do away with. Anyway, since Bonaparte no longer calls him Marshal, that vain and ridiculous pretence serves no end.'

(There is an obvious contradiction between what he says here of Bertrand and what he writes in his note. I beg your Excellency to glance at the latter.)

'You believed that I wanted to be presented at Longwood by Bertrand. That was not the case. I only wished to follow your example, to do what all your English people have done, are doing, and will do at St Helena. You see, then, that you were wrong to write me that note, which furthermore was not a reply to my letter.'

'You should, I am sure, be treated on this island just as the English are, and enjoy the same trust and liberty. The Commissioners must have access to Bonaparte, or else they will be recalled. That is my opinion. But I protest that does not depend on me. I am obeying my orders.'

'It is not, I beg you to believe, in order to renew that affair that I have taken the liberty of speaking to you about it. My desire of seeing and talking to Bonaparte does not go to the point of displeasing you. My duty at St Helena is to follow your directions in everything. But I wanted to let you know the real meaning of my letter.'

'My position toward you is really embarrassing, and yours is not agreeable. But at Longwood our position is the same. I never see Bonaparte; that may console you.'

'As for my meetings with Gourgaud, for which you reproached me in that note, kindly give me your ideas, with which I promise to conform. But I must tell you that he seeks me out everywhere, and I acknowledge that I do not like to turn away. It is humiliating. It would be more natural, it seems to me, to forbid these gentlemen following us.'

'Please do not imagine that I have ever thought of reproaching you. You conduct yourself with great propriety toward me, and Gourgaud too is a good fellow; it isn't he that I fear. But if I don't look out, Bertrand or Montholon will make trouble for you, and I haven't the same opinion of them. They are intriguers.'

'What Gourgaud told me cannot interest you. He spoke to me of his military service, of his comrades, of the battle of Waterloo.' I outlined these details, and he listened attentively, then saying:

'I have had very unpleasant scenes with Admiral Malcolm, on account of his too frequent visits to Longwood. He went so far as to send reports of them to the newspapers, unknown to me. I finally protested to the Ministry. He is a man quite without judgment.'

'Well, never shall you and I have a misunderstanding. My conduct for the last fifteen months is a guarantee of the future. But try to rid yourself of your distrust and reserve toward the Commissioners.'

'There are things which I can reveal to you; there are others which I must keep from you. The fault is not mine, but my duty's.' He then told me some old and forgotten facts, promised to send me his notes on Montholon's letter, painted another frightful portrait of Bertrand, told me that Piontkowski had tried to corrupt some officers of the garrison, and that he was still writing them some extravagant letters, but that, seeing in the Pole only an adventurer, a man without means and turned off by Bonaparte, he had taken no action.

In bringing together, Monsieur le Comte, all that the Governor has said and written on my presentation at Longwood, it cannot be denied that there are many inconsistencies in his conduct. First, he encourages me to go there unofficially. Then he opposes insurmountable obstacles. And he finally says that it is not to him but to his Government that I must apply for advice. On every occasion this is the way that he acts, and it is such conduct that has lost him all chance of getting along with Bonaparte.

I have the honour to be, etc.

No. 20

October 1, 1817.

When Bonaparte learned that the Commissioners could not, even as private individuals, see him through the intermediary of Bertrand, he became so angry that nobody dared to accost him. He remained in his room for ten days, dining alone, doing nothing, very rude to his suite. Gourgaud especially suffered the worst blows and was so affected that he spoke of suicide. 'The Emperor,' he said to me, 'is unrecognizable. When he was at the head of his armies we served him with pleasure. Today his misfortunes have soured his mind. He is another man.' Happily this storm has passed. On September 9 there was a horse-race at Longwood. A number of people were present, and Bonaparte himself, surrounded by his companions in misery, appeared on his veranda. With Mme. Stürmer I approached to within pistol-range. As soon as he perceived us, his whole entourage, including the children, came to meet us, and showered us with compliments, in full view of the Governor, his staff, and all the by-standers, and remained with us. This circumstance is rather remarkable. I then made the acquaintance of M. de Montholon, who conversed at great length about his master's affairs. Here is a summary of what he said.

He asserted that he and Count Bertrand had no desire to shut the Emperor off from the world. 'If he went out, if he saw more strangers, there would be a little variety at Longwood, and less dejection. We are drying up with melancholy. So what interest could I have in turning them away? The fact is that these gentlemen bore him. Their language and customs are intolerable to him. He prefers to be alone.'

I believe M. de Montholon is right and speaks the truth.

'The Emperor desired, and still does, to take an incognito name. He would prefer that of Malmaison, or Monsieur Muiron[42] (a colonel of whom Bonaparte was fond). As soon as he had arrived at St Helena he made the suggestion to Admiral Cockburn, and renewed it to Sir Hudson Lowe. He was always answered that it would be referred to the Ministry, and no reply has yet come. After that, if they dispute on points of etiquette, whose fault is it?'

In his note M. de Montholon declared expressly that the Emperor had decided not to take an incognito. That implies contradiction. Nevertheless the fact is true, and it has just been confirmed to me.

'The Governor is niggardly beyond belief. All the Longwood provisions are of bad quality, and in quantity are never more than the bare minimum. Often a half of them are not edible. Only this morning I had to buy a veal for the Emperor's table. We get our own money only on notes of Balcombe & Company (furnisher to Bonaparte), at £50 at a time. One day I asked for sixty and they made difficulties. At Plymouth we had 4000 napoleons. Since then the imperial silver has been taken apart* and sold at the rate of five shillings an ounce. M. de Las Cases on his departure made a loan of 4000 louis in letters of exchange. We are already about at the end of it, and all this money has served only for our needs. From that you can judge both the cost of living here and the insufficiency of the £8000 allotted to the Emperor.'

It is true that the meat is tough, the fowl very lean, the vegetables watery, all the provisions bad. But there are no others, and Longwood, as always, had the best procurable. There are 3000 men to feed and only two transports to carry rations. There should be at least six in order to have plenty. The story of the silverware, and of Las Cases's loan, is also true. But the Governor says that the maintenance of the household of Longwood costs more than £14,000 a year. All that I can say is that it is supplied in a niggardly way.

'The Governor is a tyrant, a jailer clothed with absolute power, who amuses himself with vexing us. What he thinks up every day to prevent an escape is simply ridiculous. If I go walking with you I cannot go off the highway; he would be frightened. How little he knows his prisoner!—the Emperor is not an adventurer, to throw himself into a skiff, to sail off, for what destination no one knows. In Cockburn's time we were free and could go anywhere. Bertrand signed approvals of permits for Longwood. What we needed was a Governor firm, conscious of his duty, but human, tactful, broader-minded than this one. England should be ashamed of her choice.'

The Governor is no tyrant, merely very unreasonable. He is killing his people inch by inch. His is a weak, stubborn mentality which becomes frightened at almost nothing. In short, he is such as I have always depicted him.

'Count de las Cases was arrested, taken away, they have never said why. He used to write to a Lady Clavering, his former mistress. Perhaps he used some secret means to get through a letter and to inform her in detail of what concerned him personally. It was to no purpose whatever that the Governor made such a fuss about it, for he had never any idea of escaping.

'An Englishman from Calcutta sent the Emperor a superb chess set, ornamented with Oriental figures, and on each piece there was a French eagle of marvellous workmanship.[43] The Governor did not at first see these eagles and sent in the set. When a few days later someone called his attention to it he believed himself betrayed and ruined. And then to reassure himself he wrote immediately to Bertrand and formally protested against the sending of the set. That is simply characteristic.'

The last episode is well known and is still spoken of here.

I have not failed to inform the Governor of this conversation, only toning down those parts that would offend him. He was obliged to me for my frankness, and said that Bonaparte was a spendthrift, Montholon a liar, that all his prisoners are perfectly happy. I refrained from contradicting him, but it is none the less true that his conduct toward them is a little mad, and that even the English are beginning to say so.

I have the honour to be, etc.

---

* L'argenterie imperial a été mise en pieces.—Balmain.

No. 21

October 14, 1817.

I have the honour to enclose the account which Dr O'Meara gave of the earthquake of September 21, and six bulletins from Longwood. MM. Gourgaud and Montholon have assured me that Bonaparte was suffering much, that the total lack of exercise was changing his temperament. 'Why,' I asked them, 'does he never go out or ride horseback?' 'Each time,' they told me, 'that Bertrand or we or anyone else speak of it, he answers angrily, '"Since they want to kill me, let them, and have it over with."'

The other day M. de Montholon hinted to Baron Stürmer that Bonaparte would like to see him as a private individual. 'If he were in danger of dying,' he said to Stürmer, 'and had you summoned, would you come?' This question considerably embarrassed my colleague, and he avoided answering. The Governor is terribly disturbed over his prisoner's health and does not know which way to turn. The doctors prescribe horse back riding, but the patient refuses, swears that he will never stir from his room unless they cancel the present regulations and re-establish Admiral Cockburn's. Bertrand has already obtained an extension of the limits and permission to leave the highroads and to enter private houses. I believe he will obtain the rest before long. Your Excellency will find under this cover the correspondence on the subject.

I have the honour to be, etc.

* * *

A letter from Dr O'Meara, dated September 22, 1817, gives the details of three slight earthquake shocks, and it is followed by several health bulletins.

First Letter from Count Bertrand to Sir Hudson Lowe

September 30, 1817.

I have informed the Emperor that you have done me the honour of coming to my house the day before yesterday, that you had told me you were disturbed about his health, and that, since it was attributed to lack of exercise, you wondered why he did not ride horseback. I have today the honour to repeat to you that the Emperor's existence, especially for the last six weeks, has been extremely uncomfortable; that since the month of May the Emperor has not ridden, and has rarely gone out of his apartment, and then only to visit my wife; that you know perfectly that what has prevented and still prevents the Emperor from going out is the series of restrictions of October 9, 1816, which first came into force six weeks after your arrival; that among these restrictions is the prohibition of speaking and listening to people whom he meets, and of entering any house.

You pointed out to me that you have since cancelled that part of the restrictions, which is true. But you have several times insinuated that you believe yourself authorized to re-establish them at any moment, together with any others quite as unreasonable. New restrictions which you announced on March 14, 1817, prohibit him from leaving a highway less than twelve feet wide. The result would be that the sentinels might fire on him. The Emperor cannot give in to such ignoble treatment. Several distinguished Englishmen, either now on the island or who have been here recently, not knowing of these restrictions, reproach the Emperor for sacrificing his health by not going out, but as soon as they have been informed of the facts, they admit that no man of honour could act differently, and that in a similar situation they would not conduct themselves otherwise.

I added that if you cared to consult the officers who are in this colony, you would not find one who does not regard these restrictions as unjust, useless, and oppressive. I also had the honour to remind you that under the terms of the Act of Parliament of April 11, 1816, you have not the right to make restrictions; that the Act grants such right only to the Government, which cannot delegate it, even to one of its Ministers, certainly not to a military officer; that Lord Bathurst, in his speech in the month of March, in the House of Lords, declared that you had made no new restriction, that all his correspondence had been in favour of the prisoners, and that you had the same instructions as your predecessor; that your predecessor had adapted the Government's restrictions to the local situation in a manner, if not altogether proper, at least tolerable; that things thus went on for nine months, during which time the Emperor went out, even received English officers at his table, and had had social relations with the officers and people of the island; that this order of things was not changed by an act of your Government; that during these nine months there was no unpleasantness, and that nothing can have authorized you to substitute for such a reasonable condition that which you have established; that the Emperor would go out, would ride, and would resume his old life if you put things back as they were on your arrival: that otherwise you would be responsible for the results of the restrictions, which are the equivalent for the Emperor to an absolute prohibition of leaving his apartments.

You then informed me that the Emperor's room was too small and Longwood most unsuitable, as you had pointed out to your Government, and that the Emperor having had built last year a tent, since he had no shady alley where he could walk, you proposed to put up a wooden soldier's shed, near the house, to which the Emperor could walk. When I communicated to him your proposal, he considered it as an insult (those were his very words). If the house which he now inhabits is unsuitable, why has he been left there for two years, without discovering one situated among gardens and trees, shade and water, and why has he been left on this barren spot, exposed to all the winds that blow, without anything that can contribute to make life bearable?

The Emperor added that this soldier's cabin would be of no use to him; that it could not remedy the unhealthfulness of his room and would only give him the annoyance of having workmen around; that walking under cover could never keep up one's health like exercise in the open; that it was especially horseback riding which the doctors ordered. He considers your resolution as a death sentence on your part. He is absolutely at your disposal. You are making him die of illness. You can make him die of hunger. It would be a kindness if you had him die of a rifle-shot. The doctors will tell you that there is no time to lose, that perhaps three or four weeks will be too late,[44] and although this great Prince may be abandoned by Providence and the field left clear in Europe for calumnies and slanders, yet a cry of indignation will rise from all the peoples on earth; for there are on St Helena several hundred people, French, English, and foreigners, who will set forth all that has been done to put an end to the life of this great man.

Always I have used this language to you, sir, with more or less emphasis. I shall speak to you of these things no longer, for arguments are futile. The question, then, is simply: Do you, or do you not, wish to kill the Emperor? If you persist in your conduct, you will have answered in the affirmative, and unhappily your aim will have probably been reached after a few months of agony.

In conclusion, permit me to answer, on behalf of the officers who are with the Emperor and of myself, your letters of the twenty-fifth and twenty-sixth of July last. You little know our character. Threats have no power over us. For twenty years we have braved every danger in his service. By remaining voluntarily at St Helena in our present horrible position, we are sacrificing to him more than our lives. Insensible to your threats and your insinuations, we shall continue to fulfil our duty, and if any complaint has been lodged against us with your Government, we do not doubt that the Prince Regent, Lord Liverpool, and so many other estimable men who are members of your Government will know how to judge it at its true worth; they know the respect which is due our holy mission, and in the face of persecution we shall follow our device: Fais ce que dois, advienne que pourra.

I have the honour to be, etc.

LE Cte. BERTRAND.

Reply of the Governor

October 20, 1817.

Having taken into consideration the objections which so strongly disincline General Bonaparte from taking any exercise on horseback within his present limits, I have the honour to signify to you for his information, that although for nearly six months after my arrival in this Island, when the whole of the space in the ravines between Longwood and the new road by Woody Ridge lay open to him, he never once rode in that direction, that he then only took exercise either within the grounds of Longwood or on the road by Woody Ridge, which embraces the whole circuit of his first limits, gives him the same extent of riding ground of nearly twelve miles as before, in the only part of the space which would be usually considered as practicable for horse exercise, unaccompanied by an officer; and finally, that the only real restraint which General Bonaparte is under from riding or walking over any other part of the Island, arises from his own predominant objection against permitting an English officer to accompany or be near him, I shall notwithstanding in deference to the perseverance of his opinion on a point where he exposes his own health by it, make such an arrangement as will throw open to him the whole of the space between Longwood and the new road, thus enabling him to traverse it on foot or on horseback in any direction he may choose.

The same latitude however I do not feel myself warranted in extending to the officers and other persons of his family (as the same motives do not apply to them), except at the time they may be in immediate personal attendance upon him.

I beg leave to request the honour of being informed, if General Bonaparte has accepted the offer I took the liberty to make to you of constructing a temporary wooden building in his garden, to supply the place of the tent which I had caused last year to be erected there.

I have, etc.

H. Lowe,
Lt. Genl.

(This letter crossed Count Bertrand's.—Balmain.)

Second Letter of Count Bertrand to the Governor

Longwood, October 3, 1817.

I have received yesterday at four o'clock the letter which you have done me the honour to write me under date of October 2, which crossed mine of September 30. The Emperor informs me that your letter contains restrictions more arbitrary and unjust than all the others. . . .

I have the honour to be, etc.

C$^{te.}$ BERTRAND.

Reply of the Governor

October 4, 1817.

Although I yesterday repaired to Longwood for the express purpose of removing those sentries who might be supposed most likely to interfere with General Bonaparte during the course of his walks or rides, yet in consequence of your letter of yesterday I have, to give a still farther proof of my desire to meet his view where an objection may be still supposed to exist against his taking the horse exercise which is represented as so necessary to his health, resolved not to insist upon the exclusion of the officers and other persons of his suite from the use of the space of ground designated in my letter of the 2nd when they are not in attendance upon him, but that the whole of the space shall be thrown open equally to them as to him so that there can in such case be no mistake of persons or any likelihood of interruption proceeding from such cause.

H. Lowe.

Third Letter of Count Bertrand to the Governor

October 5, 1817.

I have the honour to acknowledge receipt of your letter of October 4. Since mine of September 30, the Emperor's health has grown worse. He is feeling pain in his right side and in the shoulder, which the doctors diagnose as a beginning of the liver disease so common in this country, and which every year carries off so many people. It is, then, urgent that you should come to a decision and remove the absolute prohibition which prevents the Emperor's going out and riding horseback. Eight days have already passed in this futile correspondence.

Allow me another observation. Obliged today to communicate the original of your despatches, since the contents are too delicate for me to do otherwise, even for a translation, I notice that the expression 'General Bonaparte' keenly distressed him. Would it be agreeable to you to conform to the text of your Bill and to call him Napoleon, as your Parliament does? Furthermore, is that not an obligation for you, and, without again disobeying that Bill, can you use a title which seems to protest against the great principles of the rights of nations? Your Bill is law, and you owe it obedience, especially when by obeying your law you spare yourself an occasion of offending.

Cte. BERTRAND.

No. 22

October 20, 1817.

Bonaparte, having learned, I know not when or how, that the Governor and the Commissioners are receiving official bulletins on his health, has just forbidden Dr O'Meara, under penalty of dismissal, to communicate any of them in the future the original of which has not been previously examined, certified, and deposited at Longwood. At the same time he vigorously reprimanded him for referring to him as General, said that it was an infamy, and became very angry. Since Dr O'Meara is a very necessary man at St Helena, who is used for the indirect espionage of the French, the Governor, in order not to be deprived of his services, consented to receive no more bulletins. But none the less he will be informed, daily and in detail, of everything that concerns the health of the prisoner of Europe, so it amounts to the same thing.

Your Excellency will find enclosed five large notebooks of observations made at Longwood by Bonaparte's order, on the speech delivered by Lord Bathurst in the House of Lords on March 18, 1817. They were sent to Plantation House on the seventh of this month, sealed and addressed to Lord Liverpool. I am now engaged in making marginal notes, which I shall transmit to the Imperial Ministry as soon as possible. These observations are too declamatory and lengthy; everything is exaggerated and excessive. Yet the foundation is exact. The Governor's conduct is incomprehensible. His imagination is continually burdened with the responsibility that he carries, and he spends his life doing, redoing, and undoing.

I have the honour to be, etc.

Observations on Lord Bathurst's Speech

The *Morning Chronicle* of March 19, 1817, published the text of Lord Bathurst's speech of the preceding day, and certain excerpts, without much connecting matter, are quoted in these 'Observations,' with comment so lengthy in some cases as to extend to fifteen or sixteen manuscript columns. Some of the more interesting of these remarks are here reproduced, others are paraphrased, and some are omitted altogether.

I approve these observations and desire that they be placed under the eyes of the Sovereign and the English people.

NAPOLEON.

Longwood, October 5, 1817.

'That the Noble Lord never could discuss with a due degree of impartiality the restrictions imposed upon this prisoner, while the latter conceived restrictions of what kind soever to be inhumane and unjustifiable.'

The Act of Parliament of April 11, 1816, is neither a law nor a sentence. A law decrees only generalities; the essentials of a decree are the competence of the tribunal, examination, a hearing, confrontation, and argument. This Bill is an act of proscription similar to those of Sylla and Marius, as necessary, as just, but more barbarous. But Sylla and Marius, as consuls or dictators, had an incontestable jurisdiction over the Romans. The King of England and his people neither had nor have over Napoleon. Fifteen millions of men are the oppressors in time of peace because he commanded armies against them in time of war. But Sylla and Marius signed these acts of proscription with the still bloody point of their swords in the midst of tumult and the violence of camps; the Bill of April 11 was signed in time of peace, with the seal of a great people, in the sanctuary of 'law.' Henceforth how can the members of the English Parliament dare to blame those who proscribed Charles I and Louis XVI? At least these princes perished with a prompt and painless death.

This Bill declares, firstly, that Napoleon will be treated as if he were a prisoner of war; secondly, that the English Government will have the right to make all the restrictions which it will judge necessary. By the first stipulation they have put this Prince under the protection of the law of nations, which, being founded on the principle of reciprocity, is not a guarantee in time of peace. The second stipulation destroys even the resemblance of the guarantee which they appear to have wished to give by the first. The English Bill, after having violated everything in order to seize the person of the Prince, then its illustrious guest, delivers him over, immediately and precipitately, to all the fury of his personal enemies, animated by the basest passions. A legislative senate which gives over an individual, no matter were he the last of the human race, to injustice, can have no self-respect and disowns its sacred character.

It is asked what need had the Ministers of being invested with the right to make restrictions if the law of nations was to be their guide? One of them answered that it was in order to be authorized to accord a more liberal treatment than was customary toward prisoners of war. The observers did not lament the change; they presented the secret views of the cabinet; they had a care for the honour of their country; events have justified and still justify daily their conjectures. This great man is dying on a rock of a death gradual enough for it to appear natural: excess of cruelty unknown among nations up to this hour. This Bill is more barbarous than if, like Sylla's, it had severed at one blow the head of the proud enemy.

The right of making restrictions was granted by the Bill to the Government, which cannot delegate it. Restrictions must have the form of an Order in Council, signed by the Prince. One Minister cannot exercise it. Yet it was thus that there were adopted the four restrictions which have already been published. They were communicated to St Helena only partially, and verbally, some articles by writing, extracts from the correspondence of the Minister and as a simple act of his administration.

These four restrictions are: (1) Detention at St Helena. (2) Name imposed of General Bonaparte. (3) Prohibition of going out on the rock of St Helena unless accompanied by an officer. (4) Obligation, firstly, of writing only letters unsealed and handed to the officer charged with the command of St Helena, secondly, of receiving only open letters, which have passed under the eyes of the Minister.

These four restrictions are contrary to the law of nations; so that it is not to make the situation of the prisoners more pleasant that the Ministers have had themselves invested with the right of making restrictions. No instance in the history of either Great Britain or France can ever be cited of prisoners of war having been sent as the place of detention to another continent and a rock isolated in the midst of the oceans. If the only object was the safe-keeping of the prisoners, castles or houses are not lacking in England, but it was the devouring climate of the tropics which was needed.

The second restriction has no more connection than the first with the security of the prisoners; it has the effect of aggravating the position of the Prince. Prisoners of war when they fall into the hands of the enemy are recognized by the title which they bore in their country. 'But the Bourbons have not ceased to reign in France; the republic and the fourth dynasty were not legitimate governments.' On what are based these new principles? If the English Government maintains that the Bourbons were reigning in France at the time of the Peace of Amiens in 1802, it must recognize that Cardinal York reigned in England at the Treaty of Paris in 1753, that Charles XIII does not reign in Sweden. To consecrate these principles is to spread disorder among all monarchies, to propagate germs of revolution among all nations.

It was well known that the Emperor would never make use of the permission contained in the third restriction, so that it must have been anticipated that he would not go out of an unhealthy house. What connection can this restriction have with security, on a steep rock 600 leagues away from any continent, around which cruise several brigs, where there is only one anchorage, and the whole circumference of which can be covered by ten or twelve posts of infantry? It was also known that in order not to submit to the humiliation prescribed in this fourth restriction he would receive and write no letter. It is only possible to exchange letters between Europe and this far distant island at the most twice a year. How can such a correspondence react on the tranquillity of Europe? But it removes all moral comfort; it is to the soul what the climate of this frightful country is to the body. The end desired is being attained in two directions at once.

The officer commanding at St Helena can in theory be charged only with the execution of the restrictions; but in practice it is not so. He makes, unmakes, and remakes, alone, regulations and restrictions, fantastically, suddenly, illegally. No limit has been found to his arbitrariness, no resource against his passion, his caprice, and the folly of a single man; there is no council, no magistrate, no lawyer, no public opinion on this rock.

Does the Minister believe it is impossible that an officer appointed to the command of St Helena should abuse his power? But when he chose him *ad hoc*, and among men of a character known by their preceding missions, is it not probable that he should abuse it? And when he told him, 'If the prisoner escapes, your honour and your fortune are lost,' does that not insure abuses? A jailer in Europe cannot impose even on criminals restrictions according to the extent of his alarm, his caprice, or his passion; the matter must be referred to magistrates. . . .

When they cleverly desired to conceal the real object in their minds in choosing St Helena, they alleged: It is in order that the prisoners may enjoy more liberty. But it is quite apparent, from the restrictions, the instructions given, and the man chosen, that the real object was to prevent the cries of agony from reaching the Prince and the English people. They feared the indignation of those generous men[45] who have still some influence on the opinion of European nations.

Lord Bathurst in this speech states two things: (1) that Sir Hudson Lowe has taken only measures of execution; (2) that all the Government's communications to St Helena have been to the advantage of the prisoners. These two assertions are equally false. See Annex A, which encloses eight or nine new restrictions that would be considered dishonouring at Botany Bay. Only a few items of the Minister's correspondence are known; one letter, communicated in October by the chief of staff of the commandant, was full of improper expressions. It was ordered immediately to take three of the twelve servants who had followed Napoleon to St Helena and to send them to the Cape of Good Hope. Accordingly Captain Piontkowski and three servants were sent to the Cape. It is hinted that in turn all the French servants would have the same fate and that the only ones left with the Emperor would be those chosen by the commandant. It cannot be said that these servants gave cause for complaint, because they were not designated by name.

'That he had not received letters from his relations and friends in Europe, and that it was impossible for him to receive them. This was not true.'

To whom does this apply? Count Montholon has not complained, nor will he, about Napoleon's receiving no letters, since the latter has stated that he would receive no unsealed letter.

'As might be inferred from a letter of Sir George Cockburn to him.'

There was not, and cannot be, any correspondence between Napoleon and the officers of the English Government, since they cannot agree on the title.

'He did not know how he could discharge his duty if he did not make himself acquainted with the nature of such communications.'

The commandant of this country has been asked for an assurance that a letter to the sovereign would be sent to England unsealed. If the King of England could receive only such letters as the Ministers had previously read, England was assuredly no longer a monarchy. At Venice, Ragusa, Lucca, the doges or the *gonfalonieri* were never submitted to such humiliation. It is probable that if a Minister should open a letter addressed to the Prince without previous authorization, the Prince would remove all confidence from him; the English constitution has never impressed such a blemish on the crown of Edward or Elizabeth. The entire nation would have been branded. If ministers are responsible to legislature, kings are responsible to God and their people. Ministers are not responsible for what the prince knows, learns, or reads, but for the orders which he gives and the measures which he takes.

'On the knowledge that attempts had been made through the medium of newspapers to hold communications with Napoleon.'

Napoleon has never asked anything. On arriving at Madeira, Count Bertrand asked if they would be able to find French books, of which they had very few. He made out a list of books and asked to have it sent to a bookseller in London or Paris. Admiral Cockburn said he would take care of it. And in fact, in June, 1816, boxes of books were received, without a catalogue, without explanation. When it was perceived that there was no contemporary book, that they had even stopped the set of the *Moniteur* at 1808, Count Montholon judged proper to point out these facts for the purpose of knowing whether it was a new restriction. What shows that this new restriction has nothing novel about it, is the avowal that no papers can be sent to Longwood which are really wanted there, because 'attempts had been made,' etc. What a chimera! How can they imagine that at 2000 leagues from Europe, receiving papers so rarely, correspondence can be carried on through them? But are newspapers printed at St Helena?

It was on such pretexts that the jailers of the Inquisition and the Council of Ten at Venice used to forbid not only journals and books but even paper, ink, and light.

'The next complaint was, that he was not allowed to open a correspondence with a bookseller. Now this was not true.'

The correspondence with a bookseller could be carried on by unsealed letters. The officers correspond daily in that way with their families. But it is easy to conceive that if the *Morning Chronicle* or the *Edinburgh Review* can occasion a correspondence extremely dangerous to the safety of England, the correspondence with a bookseller is dangerous in another way. Since this dealer sends three or four hundred volumes at once, it would be necessary to go through each one, and even then are there not sympathetic ink and secret alphabets? Hence books sent by their authors, well known in London, have been held back at St Helena. [The episode of the botanist is then described.] Count de las Cases, taken away violently from Longwood in November, 1816, was held incomunicado for a month, before being sent to the Cape. Before he left the Emperor desired to see him. But the Count could receive communications which might upset Europe. At the Cape of Good Hope he had to wait several months for permission to go to Europe. He has been there for six months, and there is no indication as yet of his return.

'Who had ever heard of an affectionate draft on a banking house, or an enthusiastic order for a sale of stock?'

Where was it said that he could not even correspond with his banker or agent? Count Montholon in a letter which called forth this speech said just the opposite, and effectively answers the feeble witticism of the noble lord. He says, 'I have had the honour to tell you that the Emperor had no money.'

'That the letters sent by General Bonaparte or persons of his suite were read by subaltern officers. This was not true.'

The respect due to private correspondence has not been shown. The Minister himself acknowledges as much when he says in the face of Europe that Prince Joseph was the only one who has written the Emperor; and even that *was not true*....

[The observations are especially vehement regarding the treatment of letters and packages. Bathurst rejects with indignation the idea that letters for St Helena had been sent back to London.]

But he is indignant at the execution of his own orders; they are positive: 'No letter that comes to St Helena except through the Secretary of State must be communicated to the General or his attendants, if it be written by a person not residing in the island.' The commandant has, then, had to send back letters which did not arrive by that route, and if he had not done so he would have gone counter to his instructions. A few days ago, when he handed to Count Bertrand a case containing educational books and some children's things which Lady Holland had sent to Countess Bertrand, he first declared that this case had been addressed to him directly, that it had not passed through the office of the Secretary of State, but that he was nevertheless sending it on. If it was necessary to cite the number of letters, books, and other things which have not been handed over, on the ground of that article of the instructions, you would see that this has taken place very often. Yet it is true, as in the case just mentioned, that the commandant has taken it on himself to use his discretion, but simply according to whim, which is the worst of all.

'The complaint that all intercourse with the inhabitants was prevented was untrue.'

Communication with people of the island was carried on for the first nine months but has lately ceased entirely. People who have requested passes have been submitted to two humiliations—the necessity of giving information as to (1) what was said and done and (2) their purpose in going to Longwood.

'The additional restraints had been imposed because it was found Bonaparte was tampering with the inhabitants.'

This allegation is disposed of chiefly by a reminder that since May, 1816, Napoleon had not gone out.

[Complaints about the condition of the Longwood house occupy many pages; and the reply to the recriminations about Napoleon's private finances is very bitter. Bathurst calls attention to Napoleon's fortune, which he hints might be drawn upon if necessary to supplement the government allowance.]

Would you know what this great treasure is? It is known of every one. It consists of: the great harbor of Antwerp; that of Flushing, capable of sheltering the largest warships . . . [followed by a rhetorical and detailed enumeration, occupying nine columns, of the tremendous improvements in the aspect of Europe, from one end to the other, not only physical but cultural, which were due solely to his initiative]. All that constitutes a treasury of several billions which will exist for centuries and will forever confound calumny. History's verdict will be that it was in the midst of great wars, by means of no loan but on the contrary while lessening the public debt and reducing it to less than fifty millions, that all this was accomplished.

[Many more columns are devoted to analogies between the treatment of prisoners in all ages and countries with the barbarity practised here.]

[In connection with the complaints about finances, it would be appropriate to quote Annex F, which is a letter from Lowe to Monthalon, August 17, 1816. The other annexes are with one exception omitted as not being of sufficient general importance.]

Annex F

In pursuance of the conversations I have already had with you on the subject of the expenses of the establishment at Longwood, I do myself the honour to acquaint you that having used all efforts to effect a reduction in them without diminishing in any very sensible manner from the convenience or comfort of General Bonaparte or any of the families or individuals that form his suite (in which operation I am happy to acknowledge the spirit of concert with which you have assisted), I am now enabled to transmit to you for General Bonaparte's information two statements furnishing sufficiently precise data, whereon to found a calculation of the probable annual expense, should matters continue on the same footing as at present established.

The statement No. I has been furnished me by Mr Ibbetson, head of the commissariat department in this island.[46] The latter has been framed by my military secretary.

The instructions I have received from the British Government oblige me to limit the expenditure of General Bonaparte's establishment to £8000 per annum. They give me liberty at the same time to admit of any further expense being incurred, which he may require, as to table and so forth, beyond what this sum would cover, provided he furnishes the funds whereby the surplus charge may be defrayed.

I am now therefore under the necessity of requesting you would make known to him the impossibility I am under of bringing the expenses of his household on its present establishment in point of numbers, within the limits prescribed, unless I make such a reduction under several heads as might materially abridge from the conveniences which the persons around him enjoy; and having been already very frankly informed by him as well as by yourself that he has at his disposal in various parts of Europe means whereby the extra or even the whole expense may be defrayed* I beg leave to request being informed, previous to attempting any further considerable reduction which might prove inconvenient to him or to the persons of his suite, if he be content such an attempt should be made, or if he be willing to place at my command sufficient funds to meet the extra charges which must otherwise be unavoidably incurred.

H. Lowe,
Lt. General.

---

* This part of Sir Hudson Lowe's letter has already been answered by the postscript to the letter of August 23. It was stated to him that if we had the right of free correspondence and could inform Europe of the distress which we were undergoing, millions from the various countries of Europe would be offered.—Balmain.

Commissary Ibbetson's statement, 'showing the probable annual expenditure on account of General Bonaparte and suite,' amounts to a total of £19,152 2s. 7d. The largest single item is £11,700, 'supplied from government stores sent from England by Mr Balcombe, purveyor. . . . Wines, claret, grave, champagne, madeira, house and table expenses.' Not included in this budget is 'salary to Surgeon O'Meara, attached to Gl. Bonaparte and suite, not yet defined.'

Annex H
Letter from Napoleon to Count de las Cases

This letter, relating occurrences which were only too painfully familiar to its recipient, seems to be clearly intended for political effect, but as letters dictated by the Emperor himself from St Helena are not numerous in this collection and in fact do not exist in any great number, it seems worthwhile to include it.

* * *

December 11, 1816.

My heart goes out to you in what you are experiencing. Torn from my side two weeks ago, you have been kept in secrecy since that time, without my being able to give or to receive any news, without your being able to communicate with anyone either French or English, deprived even of a servant of your choosing.

Your conduct at St Helena has been like your entire life, honourable and without reproach.

Your letter to your friend at London is not blameworthy; you unbosomed yourself in the intimacy of friendship. That letter is not unlike eight or ten others which you have written the same person and which you sent unsealed. The commandant, having had the delicacy to spy on the expressions which you confided to friendship, has reproached you for them, and recently has threatened to send you from the island if your letters contained further complaints against him. Thus he has gone counter to the first duty of his situation, the first article of his instructions, and the first sentiment of honour. Consequently he has by implication authorized you to seek means of inspiring your friends with your sentiments and of informing them of the culpable conduct of this commandant. But you were naïve, it was easy to take advantage of your confidence.

They were seeking a pretext to seize your papers, but your letter to your friend could not have authorized a police raid on your rooms, since it contains no plot or mystery, being merely the expression of a noble and candid spirit. The illegal and precipitate conduct of which they were guilty in this house bears the trace of a personal hatred which is very vile.

In countries less civilized, exiles, prisoners, even criminals, are under the protection of laws and magistrates; those set over them are important administrative and judicial officials. On this rock the man who makes the most absurd regulations, and executes them with cruelty, violates all laws, and no one knows the limits of his passion.

Longwood is surrounded with a mystery which they would like to make impenetrable, in order to hide this criminal conduct. By means of rumours cleverly spread about, they seek to mislead officers, travellers, inhabitants, even the agents whom it is said Austria and Russia are maintaining on this island; no doubt they are even deceiving the English Government by these adroit and lying tales.

With ferocious joy they seized your papers (among which it was known were several that belonged to me), without any formality, in the room next mine. I was advised of it a few moments afterwards; I leaned out of my window and saw that they were taking you away; a large number of officers were prancing around the house; and it reminded me of nothing so much as South Sea islanders dancing around the prisoners whom they were about to devour.

Your company was essential to me. You alone speak, read, and understand English. Nevertheless I beseech you, and if necessary order you, to require the commandant to send you to the Continent. He cannot refuse, since he has as his only hold over you the voluntary act which you signed. It will be for me a great comfort to know that you are on the road to more fortunate countries. When you arrive in Europe, whether you go to England or return to the fatherland, forget the memory of the evils which they have inflicted on you; extol the fidelity which you have shown me and all the affection which I bear you.

If some day you see my wife and son, embrace them; for two years I have had no news of them, either direct or indirect. There has been here for six months a German botanist who saw them in the gardens of Schön-brunn a few months before his departure; the barbarians have carefully prevented him from coming to give me news of them.

My body is in the power of my enemies' hatred; they neglect nothing of what can gratify their vengeance, they are killing me by inches. But the unhealthfulness of this devouring climate and the lack of everything that can keep up life will soon, I feel, put an end to this existence, the very last moments of which will be an act of opprobrium for the English character, and some day Europe will point out with horror this astute and evil man. Real Englishmen will disavow him as a Briton.

As everything leads me to think that you will not be allowed to see me before your departure, receive my embraces, the assurance of my esteem and my friendship. Be happy!

NAPOLEON.

* * *

Every report from now on transmits a bulletin on Napoleon's health.

* * *

No. 23

November 2, 1817.

I have the honour to transmit to your Excellency a bulletin from Longwood signed by Baxter,[47] Inspector-General of Hospitals. Since the fourteenth of last month Dr O'Meara has not dared to issue any bulletin. Bonaparte is most obstinate in forbidding him to do so. But the two doctors have been ordered to confer on the state of his health, and Baxter makes the report to the Governor.

General Gourgaud, whom I saw this morning, assured me that Bonaparte was becoming melancholy and was gradually falling into a complete apathy. 'He works no longer on his history. He has given up everything and does nothing but idle. For five weeks he has been dining alone, lives constantly alone, and talks only of his death. Yesterday he painted us a picture of his misery which wrung my heart. I could scarcely keep back my tears.'

I have also seen Count Montholon, who said the same thing. 'Why do you not come to Longwood to lighten our burden a little? The Emperor strongly praised your conduct during the first year. It was prudent. Not knowing the terrain, nor the people, you could not have done better than to temporize. But after all the advances he has made to you, you have carried your reserve too far. Have they told you to avoid him, or do you depend entirely on the whims of the Governor? The Emperor charges me to tell you that if he were your sovereign he would disapprove, for nothing can prevent you from being courteous.'

I said nothing.

'Longwood,' he resumed smiling, 'complains of your indifference but holds no grudge against you for it. They will always receive you with open arms, as well as M. and Mme. Stürmer and Captain de Gors. As for M. de Montchenu, we will have none of him. He retails ridiculous stories about us and fills the newspapers with them. The Emperor feels insulted by him and refuses to see him, not as an émigré, a subject of Louis XVIII, but as a culumniator.'

I have the honour to be, etc.

P.S. The last trunk from London brought us a pamphlet entitled 'Manuscrit Venu de St Hélène d'une Manière Inconnue.'[48] As it is attracting great attention in Europe and throws much light on past events, I am trying to discover its author. M. de Montholon declared to me positively that it did not come from Longwood. In fact this work, being filled with anachronisms, cannot emanate from Count de las Cases. On reading it Bonaparte said, 'it is not by me, but by someone who knows me well.' That is all I know of it at present.

No. 24

November 10, 1817.

I have received the letter which your Excellency has done me the honour to send me, dated St Petersburg, April 5 last. The salary which the Emperor deigns to grant me is quite sufficient for my needs. With £2000 a year, and an allowance of £1600 I have enough to pay my debts and live quite decently. Be willing, Monsieur le Comte, to lay at his Majesty's feet the homage of my gratitude. I am deeply sensitive of the value of his benefits and aspire only to the happiness of pleasing him, of deserving his approval, and of being useful to the service. But, I cannot repeat too often, my position in that respect is very embarrassing. The English Government, or rather the Governor, is decidedly opposed to my being presented to Bonaparte. They are even alarmed at my meeting people at Longwood. In short, they do not wish me to see things close up, because national vanity would suffer. Being thus harassed, watched over on all sides, drawn forward by the French and kept back by the English, I am managing as well as possible between these two opposites, and scarcely dare to move.

My health continues bad. I suffer much from nerves, and this climate weakens them. St Helena is really unhealthy. The doctors are not of the opinion that I should stay twenty months longer. But I submit without murmur to the Emperor's will and am ready to sacrifice my life to him.

I have the honour to be, etc.

St Helena, November 17, 1817.

I have the honour to inform your Excellency that Napoleon Bonaparte suffered a good deal from Toothache on the night of the 15th instant, and in consequence was at last induced to permit Mr O'Meara to extract the dent sapientie of the right side of the upper Jaw. This is the first surgical operation that has ever been performed upon his body. The tooth was carrious in two places. In other respects his health continues much the same as in my last report.

I have, etc.
Alex Baxter,
D. G. of Hos.

True Copy.
H. Lowe.

No. 27

December 13, 1817.

I have the honour to send two bulletins from Longwood.

Bonaparte's liver is seriously affected, and his health is visibly deteriorating. The devouring air of the tropics, his excessive leisure, are altering his blood and his temperament. At night he does not sleep. In the daytime he is torpid. His complexion is livid, his eyes sunken. His condition excites pity. Dr O'Meara told me confidentially that he did not give him more than two years of life. Only exercise can bring him back. But he will take none, I am willing to guess, as long as Sir Hudson Lowe will be Governor of St Helena.

I have the honour to be, etc.

No. 28

December 31, 1817.

The last few days Bonaparte has spoken only of our August Master. He has told Mme. Bertrand some stories of the interview of Tilsit, of the lovely Queen of Prussia, and other similar anecdotes. He seems to like the Emperor and says often; 'I was very foolish not to go to Russia. I shall repent of it eternally.' He is angry that I cannot see him, for he is disposed to place confidence in me and to communicate to me some very interesting things. One day he wanted to give me his version of the battle of Waterloo. They had already made a copy for me. But whether he feared to alarm the Governor or whether he suddenly changed his mind, as often happens, he shut up the original and the copy in his desk and spoke no more of it.

There is a serious misunderstanding between Sir Hudson Lowe and Dr O'Meara. The latter, disgusted with the Governor's undue sensitiveness and instability, has ceased to see him, and informs him no longer of what is happening at Longwood. The Governor asked him the reason, and, as is often the case, used threats. The other answered shortly that he was a doctor, not a spy. I have all this from Dr O'Meara himself. 'Sir Hudson Lowe,' he told me, 'does not walk straightly or sincerely. One can have nothing to do with him, for one is never sure of what he says or writes.'

I was anxious to transmit this opinion to you because this testimony of an Englishman, and of an Englishman who is in a position to see everything, and whom nothing seems to escape, could not be suspect, and is more convincing than mine.

I have the honour to be, etc.

* * *

From now on O'Meara and his intrigues play a very important rôle in these reports, and it is most interesting, and a little amusing, to watch Balmain's gradual change of attitude toward him.

Barry O'Meara was well bred and well educated. He was hardly thirty years old when he first entered Napoleon's service, and that helps to explain him and to introduce the two motives which, at least in the beginning, were the compelling ones: curiosity and ambition. His position was a false one from the start. Napoleon wished this young man, constantly in attendance upon him and dependent on his generosity, to do for him many things which his followers could not do because they were not free to come and go. To be sure, they were not very serious errands—the carrying of newspapers and letters, for instance—but they were prohibited things. To some extent the young doctor also saved the governor's face, since he could watch Napoleon's actions without seeming to do so and hence hurting his feelings. The fact that he was mutually useful in this way is shown by the regulation drawn up after his departure requiring Napoleon to show himself to the orderly officer twice daily. But all that was hardly the duty of a physician.

Things might have gone on thus until the end had not O'Meara begun his correspondence with John Finlaison, an old friend of his who was keeper of the records at the Admiralty, in London. Who could have supposed such letters to remain 'confidential'? When Finlaison asked if he might show this fascinating and important correspondence to the Admiralty, O'Meara consented, thinking, perhaps sincerely, that the lords of the Admiralty would be glad to have confidential information of an unofficial character, but incidentally hoping that his superior officers would be thereby impressed with the merits of the writer. Loyal to neither Lowe nor Napoleon, he finally came to the conclusion that his ambition required preference to be given to the fallen hero. Says Gonnard, 'His was a concentrated, violent nature, capable of deep hatred.' He seems for some time to have won Balmain over rather completely, and the Russian allowed himself to be persuaded that the Longwood news had only been given to Lowe as a topic of conversation and that O'Meara had always behaved in a perfectly straightforward manner.

A Fantastic Project of Escape

The question as to whether escape was ever possible for Napoleon comes up seldom in connection with these reports. Balmain during his entire sojourn seems to have heard of only one plan actually concocted, that of Colonel Latapie. A search through the St Helena literature would, of course, produce vast quantities of talk and rumour but hardly any project which got even so far as this one.

Was escape possible? One has only to read the accounts in these reports of the infinite precautions taken by Lowe to answer in the negative.[49] Many authorities believe that, even if it were possible, it would not have been attempted. A vessel of large size would have been immediately detected and could not have withstood the cruisers on permanent guard around the island. However, as Norwood Young points out, a whaler or small merchant vessel (or a dinghy from a ship lying to at a great distance, provided the weather were foggy) might possibly have approached the shore at night unobserved, and Napoleon could, with a little luck, have got down to the beach. If no vessel was then at hand he might have found a cave, or a rock, for concealment until a boat put in. The vessel would have had to evade the cruisers and arrive at the designated point precisely at the time appointed.

What then, if he succeeded; and what if he failed? He said to O'Meara: 'Where could I go? Everywhere I should find enemies to seize me.' If the world still feared Napoleon, he was hardly in less terror of the world. And in case of failure he was fully convinced that he would be shot. His indifference to escape was not, however, realized until the time when his health began definitely to fail.

THE YEAR 1818

No. 1

January 1, 1818.

The sloop of war *Blossom* arrived this morning from Brazil, bringing the Governor a packet of despatches from the English Chargé d'Affaires at Rio de Janeiro and some letters from my Lord Bathurst. M. de Montchenu has received by the same mail a letter, a copy of which I have the honour to send your Excellency. He hastened to have it read to Sir Hudson Lowe. But the latter, far from communicating to us those of Mr Chamberlain, frowned on our even speaking of them to him, and says not a word. This conduct is really indecent.

I have the honour to be, etc.

* * *

According to the letter from M. de Maler, French chargé d'affaires and consul-general in Brazil, dated Rio, December 3, 1817, two men had arrived at Pernambuco on the Portuguese vessel *Rainha*, and were immediately arrested by the governor, who suspected that they had come to take part in a rebellion there. One of these adventurers proved to be Colonel Latapie, who acknowledged that he was a Bonapartist. The other was an Austrian who had been a captain in the French cavalry. Sent to Rio, they were examined by the minister of state, Senhor Bezerra, who was so intrigued by the mystery surrounding them that he undertook to set them at liberty if they would explain their errand. The colonel then acknowledged the part they intended to play in the Pernambuco revolt, which with other Frenchmen they had come to aid, and then, after having established themselves in Brazil, they would use that country as the base for an expedition to St Helena. 'A large number of his comrades,' wrote M. de Maler, 'would gladly lay down their lives in the execution of this project, according to the colonel; they thought and dreamed of nothing else, and since they owed their all to the prisoner of St Helena, they would surmount all obstacles to rescue him.

Latapie refused to consider the project difficult, holding that anything was possible for such bold men, that they would surprise the garrison, that the first and only concern would be to see that Bonaparte escaped, while the assailants were fighting and being killed. He said that in order to succeed in landing on the island and eluding the vigilance of the cruiser and the lookouts, they had prepared several small steamboats which would be placed together on larger vessels, and these little boats would be put in the water at the proper distance in order to gain one of the capes of the island.

I hastened to see Senhor Bezerra, who confirmed the whole story.

Marquis d'Osmond, French ambassador to the Court of St James's, wrote from London on September 11 a warning of Colonel Latapie's attempt. His information was to the effect that the rescuers would try to seize the Portuguese islet of Fernando Noronha and there would incite a revolt among the two thousand prisoners of the penal station, who were, he said, guarded by a very weak garrison. With that help, the expedition against St Helena might become dangerous.

* * *

No. 2

January 8, 1818.

At the beginning of last October, the Governor, as I have already reported to you, extended the limits of Longwood and gave the French more liberty. Since then he has relaxed on several other points. He has allowed Bonaparte to go out of his enclosure without being accompanied by an English officer, but under the express condition that he should advise him, the night before, of the place where he wanted to go. He has also offered to add to the residence the land of Miss Mason, which is only a mile away and where there is shade. In short, all was going beautifully when Bertrand represented that in the days of Admiral Cockburn invitations and other notes of the Emperor for travellers, officers, inhabitants, were delivered to their destination sealed, and asked that that status should be re-established. That again disturbed the affairs of Longwood, for the Governor rejected this proposition, and as they answered his refusal tartly, he lost patience and threatened Bertrand with expulsion. Then Bonaparte, carried away with anger and spite, declared positively that he would not stir from his room, and wrote on the back of Sir Hudson Lowe's last letter a marginal note, which I quote, and which puts an end to these debates:

> This letter, those of July 26 and October 26, are full of lies. I have shut myself up in my apartment for eighteen months in order to have shelter from the outrages of this officer. Today my health is weakened; it no longer permits me to read such disgusting writings. Send me no more of them. Whether this officer believes himself authorized by secret and verbal instructions of his Minister, as he has allowed it to be understood, or whether he is acting on his own initiative, which might be deduced from the care he takes to disguise himself, I can only treat him as my assassin. If they had sent to this country a man of honour, I should have experienced at least some unhappiness, but they would have spared themselves the reproaches of Europe and of history, which this astute man's rubbish-heap of writings cannot deceive.
>
> November 23, 1817.

I venture to add to this report my own notes on the Observations on Lord Bathurst's speech.

I have the honour to be, etc.

Notes on the 'Observations'

'Name imposed on General Bonaparte.' After great and eternal debates on this harassing subject, the Governor has consented no longer to qualify Bonaparte as General. But he calls him Napoleon Bonaparte simply, and that is as displeasing. 'Bonaparte,' M. de Montholon said to me one day, 'without being Emperor of the French, is and always will be the Emperor Napoleon, as a bishop is still a bishop although he no longer has a bishopric, and a general remains a general although deprived of his command, or even out of service.'

'But it is the devouring climate of the tropics that was needed.' Bonaparte, who perhaps judges every one's principles and sentiments by his own, is firmly convinced that they have sent him to a rock, five hundred leagues from any land, simply to make him die by inches. No one can ever rid him of this idea.

'All the French who wish to return to their country must first run these dangers and undergo this excessive fatigue.' Mme. Bertrand told me that she would like to return to Europe to educate her children; but that she shuddered at the very idea of those three frightful voyages.[50]

'Attempts had been made through the medium of newspapers to hold communications with Bonaparte.' They say that in the papers of Count

St Helena from the Sea. This and the following five illustrations are taken from a set of aquatints drawn by George Hutchins Bellasis, and published 1 November 1815.

The Roads, St Helena, with a glimpse of Jamestown at the entrance to the Jamestown valley.

Scene taken from the castle terrace, Jamestown.

Plantation House, the country residence of the governor.

The Friar Rock in Friar's Valley.

Lot's Column, Fairy Land, Sandy Bay.

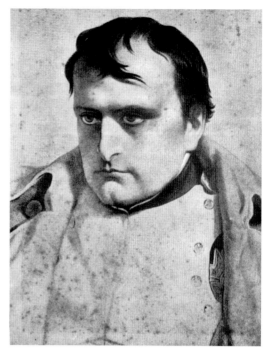

Above left: Henry, Earl Bathurst, (1762–1834). Bathurst was Secretary of State for War and Colonies, 1812–1827.

Above right: Napoleon Bonaparte, (1769–1821). A portrait of Napoleon in 1815.

Below left: Admiral Sir George Cockburn, (1772–1853).

Below right: Governor Mark Wilks, (1760–1831). Governor of St Helena from June, 1813, to April, 1816.

Above left: General Henri Gratien Comte de Bertrand, (1773–1844). Count Bertrand remained with Napoleon throughout the captivity. In 1840 he was chosen by the French Government, following agreement with the British Government to bring Napoleon's remains to France—*le retour des cendres*.

Above right: Emanuel Auguste Dieudonné Marius Joseph Marquis Las Cases, (1776–1842. Las Cases was arrested on 25 November 1816 by Sir Hudson Lowe and deported on 30 December 1816 together with his son.

Below left: Charles Tristan Comte de Montholon, (1783–1853). Count Montholon remained with Napoleon throughout the captivity.

Below right: Louis Marchand, (1792–1876). Marchand was First Valet to Napoleon at Longwood and executor to his will. His mother was nurse to Napleon's son, the King of Rome. He remained throughout the captivity and returned in 1840 for the exhumation and *le retour des cendres*.

Above left: Lieutenant-General Sir Hudson Lowe, (1769–1844). Governor of St Helena from April, 1816 to July 1821.

Above right: Charles Bayne Hodgson Ross, (1778–1849). Captain of HMS *Northumberland.*

Below left: Sir Thomas Reade, (1785–1849). Deputy Adjutant-General in St Helena.

Below right: Major Gideon Gorrequer, (1781–1841). Aide-de-Camp and Acting Military Secretary to Sir Hudson Lowe.

Above left: William Balcombe, (1779–1829). Superintendent of Public Sales under the East India Company, and Purveyor to Longwood. In addition to his official position with the East India Company, he was a merchant in partnership with William Fowler and Joseph Cole, the principal business of the firm being that of purveyors to the various ships touching at Jamestown.

Above right: Mrs Jane Balcombe. Napoleon remarked that Mrs Balcombe reminded him of Joséphine.

Below left: Betsy (Lucia Elizabeth) Balcombe, (1802–1871). Younger daughter of William Balcombe, and friend of Napoleon.

Below right: Miss Laura Wilks, (1797–1888). Daughter of Colonel Wilks. In company with her father, Miss Wilks was received by Napoleon on several occasions, and was much complimented by him on her beauty and personal charm. Laura left the island with her father in April 1816.

Above left: Major Charles Robert George Hodson, (1779–1858). Major of the St Helena Regiment, and Judge Advocate.

Above right: Maria Hodson, (1780–1863). Wife of Charles Hodson, and a daughter of Sir W. Doveton. The Hodsons lived at 'Maldivia,' close to 'The Briars,' and it was here that Napoleon paid two visits.

Below left: Mary Moore Casamajor Skelton, (1775–1866). Wife of John Skelton, (1763–1841), who had been Lt-Governor of St Helena from 1813 to 1816. Mrs Skelton was a good friend of Napoleon.

Below right: Reverend Richard Boys, (1785–1867). Chaplain to the Honourable East India Company in St Helena from 1811 to 1830.

Above left: Barry Edward O'Meara, (1782–1836); Medical Attendant to Napoleon until 25 July 1818 when Lowe caused him to be removed.

Above right: John Stokoe, (1775-1852); Surgeon to the *Conqueror*. Stokoe was summoned to attend Napoleon 17 January 1819 and over the next four days paid five visits incurring the displeasure of Lowe.

Below left: Thomas Shortt, (1788–1843); Principal Medical Officer in St Helena. He arrived at the island in December 1820 and was consulted on Napoleon's illness, He attended the post-mortem.

Below right: Archibald Arnott MD, (1771–1855); Surgeon to the 20th Foot Regiment. Arnott had excellent relations with Napoleon who gave him a gold snuff box. He attended Napoleon in his last days and attended the post-mortem.

Above left: William Crokat, (1789–1879). Orderly Officer, Longwood, 15 April to 7 May 1821.

Above right: Lt-Colonel John Mansel, (1778–1863). In command of the 53rd Foot Regiment.

Below left: Rodolphus Hobbs Reardon, (1790–1847). Lieutenant in the 66th Regiment.

Below right: Rear-Admiral Robert Plampin, (1762–1834). Commander-in-Chief of the St Helena and Cape of Good Hope Naval Stations from July 1817 to July 1820.

A view of James Town from the road leading to the Briars. The church of St James, built in 1774, gained a spire in 1843, but this was demolished in 1980 on the grounds of safety. This view would have been similar to that seen by Napoleon. This is one of a series of views published in 1857 by G. W. Melliss.

This view from T. E. Fowler's 1863 book on St Helena shows that new buildings had sprung up between the battery and St James's Church. The castelletated front has changed with the insertion of a new battery. This view shows more clearly the second line of defence, with a high wall behind the trees.

The Briars, at the head of the Jamestown valley, home of the Balcombe family, and later of Admiral Plampin. The pavilion on the mound to the right of the engraving was Napoleon's home on St Helena, October to December 1815 while Longwood was being prepared for him.

The races on Deadwood Plain, a watercolour by Denzil Ibbetson, (1788–1857), the Commissary in St Helena. Ibbetson sailed on board HMS *Northumberland* and remained on the island throughout Napoelon's captivity.

Above: An engraving of Longwood, date unknown. The illustration is something of a mystery as it shows a wooden outbuilding and a masonry wall not shown on other illustrations. It appears in Jacques Bainville's *Napoleon*, 1932. A building looking like a watchtower is to the left, apparently with a flag flying. Longwood appears in a dilapidated state and it may be mid-nineteenth century when the building was used as a granary.

Below left: A plan of Napoleon's garden as it was in 1821. Key: 1) Longwood Old House (where Napoleon lived; 2) General Bertrand's cottage; 3) The New House, where Napoleon did not live long enough to move to; 4) The stables; 5) British officers' guard house; 6) tent on the lawn; 7) vegetable garden of Noverraz; 8) Garden of Ali, (Louis Etienne Saint Denis), the librarian at Longwood House the librarian at Longwood; 9) Garden of Louis Marchand.

Below right: Napoleon in his garden. Towards the end when he threw his enthusiasm into his garden, he abandoned his bicorn cocked hat with cockade, and adopted a straw hat and canvas trousers.

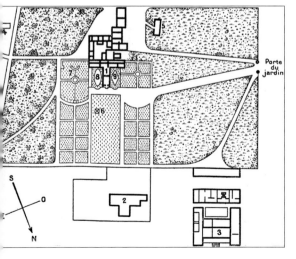

Above: A watercolour painting presumably by Louis Marchand, Napoleon's valet. This painting was offered to Napoleon 1 January 1820 and appears to be reasonably faithful depiction of the garden Napoleon created. At the far back of the garden is the tall turf wall Napoleon had built. Given Sir Hudson Lowe's antagonism, it is somewhat surprising that he was allowed to get away with it.

Below: A watercolour by Denzil Ibbetson. He remained on the island until June 1823, so presumably this painting was executed between May 1821 and June 1823. It attributes the various chambers of the house and adds: 'the House in which Napoleon died . . . which is now a granary'. In the turf wall is the spy hole cut for Napoleon to use for his telescope.

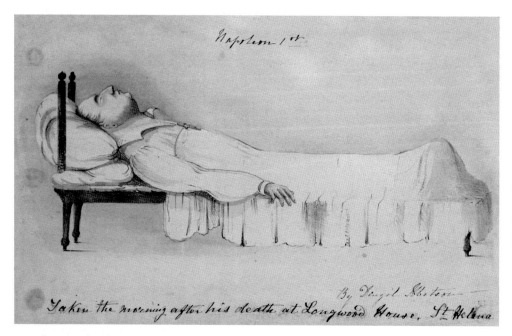

Napoleon on his death bed by Denzil Ibbetson. Napoleon died of a stomach ulcer with cancerous complications.

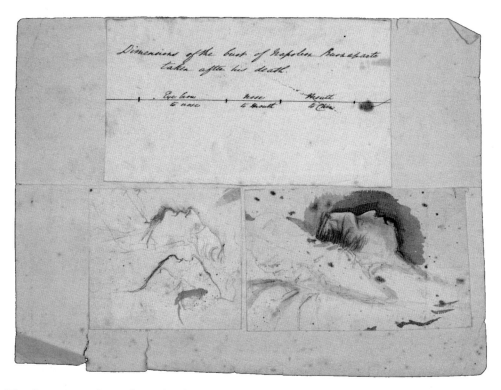

The dimensions of Napoleon's head recorded by Denzil Ibbetson.

las Cases a project has been discovered of correspondence through newspapers, but it was not carried out. It is morally impossible.

Regarding the placing of guards: At night the Longwood pavilion is surrounded with sentries. They are at the trees, at the doors and windows. M. de Montholon told me that he could see at least thirty from his room. When Bonaparte's evening is over, the French cannot cross the courtyard and make a step outside without being followed by a soldier, and General Gourgaud has assured me that he always presented his bayonet. From Longwood to the port of St James it is less than six miles, and I have counted three officers' posts, three sub-officers', and fifteen men. The other roads and paths of the island are guarded the same. More than one third of the garrison daily does sentry duty. You stumble on them in the most unexpected places. They are posted on the high rocks, and since my arrival the strong wind has knocked over four or five.

If I were charged with guarding Bonaparte, the entire island would be his domain. By day, I would submit him to no direct surveillance. I would post all my guards on the coasts. The pleasure of walking would be infinitely increased, since no soldiers would be seen, nor anything that can sadden or humiliate a prisoner. In the evening I would establish at rifle-range from Longwood a cordon of troops, which nobody would pass without my knowledge. Any other measure of security in the interior of the island is useless and vexatious. The essential point about this rock, which is unapproachable and is only ten leagues in circumference, is to guard the coasts and the sea.

. . . I asked the Governor why they did not establish the French at Plantation House. He told me: 'It is because those people would damage it too much. The upkeep of the house, the garden, and the farms costs much money. It is a superb establishment, and it would mean too much loss for the India Company. Then,' he added, 'I should have to live at Longwood. Lady Lowe is not very well, and I will never sacrifice my wife's health to Bonaparte's whims.' . . . Bonaparte insists on dislodging the Governor and demands Plantation House with all the insistence characteristic of him. I believe he will finally succeed.

I have the honour, etc.

No. 3

January 15, 1818.

Mr Farquhar, Governor of the Île de France, *en route* to London on leave, arrived at St Helena on the third and left on the eighth. He was extremely anxious for an interview at Longwood, and like all his compatriots made the customary visit to Count Bertrand. But the latter, not being willing even to announce him to Bonaparte, answered him shortly that the

Emperor was ill, out of sorts, disgusted, and received no one. This answer humiliated Mr Farquhar and intensely displeased Sir Hudson Lowe.

During the last four months Bonaparte has twice changed his ways of living. In October and November he dined at half-past nine and went to bed at ten. Now he dines at three and has only one meal a day. On Sundays he invites the French to dine. On other days he dines alone, and as he no longer holds any soirées, Mmes. Bertrand and Montholon see him very seldom. In the night his valet Marchand reads to him, and he spends half the night in bed, half in a warm bath. In the daytime, when he feels energetic enough, he writes, plays chess, tries a little of everything, but really does nothing, yawns, and kills time.

In my notes on Montholon's letter of August 23, 1816. I said that Bonaparte read all the newspapers, that they sent him all that came. This information I had from the English authorities. But I found afterward that they gave him neither French papers nor those of the Opposition in England, with the exception of a few selected issues of the *Morning Chronicle*. This only irritated him the more.

It is said in Europe that Lord Amherst had given the Prince Regent a letter from Bonaparte. That is false. There has been no letter sent from Longwood except that to Lord Liverpool, which I mentioned in my report No. 22. 'The Emperor,' Bertrand said to me, 'has a proud and lofty soul. He is consistent in his opinions, and having once complained of the Prince Regent, he will not lower himself to write him. It is to the Emperor Alexander, if the occasion presented itself, that he would write of his misfortunes, for he admires that Prince. He has great confidence in his help and thinks him endowed with fine qualities.' Bertrand tried to insinuate to me that they would gladly give me a letter for our august Sovereign. But I feigned not to guess his thought. However, Napoleon did not have a long interview with Lord Amherst on the affairs of Longwood. He described to him the character of the Governor, had him read his correspondence and the restrictions of October 9, 1816. 'If you were in my place,' he asked him, 'would you go out, would you see people? What would you do? Speak frankly, as a man of honour.' Count Montholon assured me that the noble lord answered, 'I would do as you are doing.'

When Bonaparte was told about the affair of Colonel Latapie, he refused to believe a word of it and said, 'It is a fable that they have invented to give more authority to the vexations of Sir Hudson Lowe.'

I have the honour, etc.

* * *

Gourgaud's Quarrel with Montholon and His Departure

The reports for the next few weeks are occupied for the most part with details of the growing unpleasantness between Gourgaud and Montholon. When the former, feeling that he was being worsted in the quarrel and that Napoleon was withdrawing his favour, asked permission to leave the island, the Emperor replied, 'It isn't worth the trouble, my friend. Have a little patience. Twelve months more, and you will bury me.'

In February the quarrel had reached the extent of a challenge sent by Gourgaud, which Montholon by Napoleon's orders was obliged to decline. The Emperor naturally feared the effect which such dissension, carried to the point of a duel, would have in Europe; but apparently Montholon resented his master's restriction. Gourgaud, having left Longwood, was given by the Governor a little country house near Plantation House, and there he resided until his departure.

Balmain adds, on February 15: 'The Bonapartist plots at Pernambuco have greatly excited the Governor. He works incessantly on the fortifications, is placing new telegraph posts and batteries in various places, and has doubled the guard at Longwood. I see him always on horseback, surrounded by engineers, and galloping in all directions. One cannot blame him for his extreme vigilance, but he is pushing it quite too far and is becoming ridiculous, for there is no real danger. What more could he do if he were in the presence of the enemy? One essential thing, which he scarcely seems to think of, is the provisioning of the troops. For about a month the soldiers have been on half-rations of bread, and the horses have no more forage. We lack everything on this rock and get along as if in the enemy's country, living from day to day; and it does not seem to disturb him at all, because he has only one idea in his head—the guarding of Bonaparte.'

Balmain quotes Gourgaud's first letter to Montholon, full of self-pity, devotion to the Emperor, and hatred for the man who has sowed dissension between them:

> Forced to leave the Emperor, to whom I have sacrificed my whole existence, I will go only after having avenged myself on the success of your plots. Or else I shall perish, but at least in a manner more honourable and worthier a real man than that which you have shown up to now; and whatever be my fate, I shall carry with me the esteem of all good people.

When it became apparent that Montholon could not, if he would, meet Gourgaud's wishes, the latter wrote a farewell letter to Napoleon, which the Emperor answered as follows:

I thank you for the sentiments which you express to me in your letter of yesterday. I regret that the disease of the liver which is so fatal in this climate necessitates your departure. You are young. You have talent. You are to enjoy a long career. I wish it to be happy. Never doubt the interest which I take in you.

Balmain reports a conversation between Napoleon and Gourgaud, of which he was told by Bertrand. 'I have served you,' Gourgaud said, 'with zeal and fidelity. I have sacrificed to you my liberty and my entire existence. And you abandon me.'

'Bah,' replied the other, 'what are your losses, your misfortunes? Your lot is happy. I have lost my empire, my glory. *There* are reverses for you, and I say nothing. But you are soft and weak. You make me pity you.'

Naturally Gourgaud then became desperate, and in turn blamed all those who were in better favour, going as far as to challenge first Bertrand, then Las Cases, then Montholon. It was finally thought that he was losing his mind. The more Napoleon and his suite snubbed him, the more Lowe praised him, but Balmain is sure that that was only because Gourgaud was so docile and pliable.

On March 14 Balmain wrote:

General Gourgaud left this morning for England and was not first sent to the Cape of Good Hope, which is a mark of great favour. It is said at St Helena that he has a secret mission from Bonaparte, that his trouble-making at Longwood was pure comedy, a clever way of taking in the English. I am not of that opinion. Gourgaud knows little of men and less of their ways.

Gourgaud's financial troubles occupy much space. When he left the island he had only seventeen pounds. 'Bonaparte offered him a gift of five hundred, which he refused, saying, "I will owe his Majesty only his pension of twelve thousand francs, which will serve for the needs of my family." "Those five hundred pounds," he told me, "are too little for my needs and not enough for my honour. The Emperor gave as much to his groom and to the valets who returned to France; Las Cases got two hundred thousand francs. You might remind Bertrand that I am in a position to play the Emperor a scurvy trick if I were so inclined, that I could reveal a good many secrets. My Longwood diary would be worth fifteen thousand pounds in London, and he had better not go too far."'

Of Gourgaud Bonaparte said to Bertrand: 'Speak to me no more of that man; he is mad. He was jealous, in love with me. *Que diable,* I am not his wife and can't sleep with him. I know he will write these things against me, but I don't care. If he is received in France, he will be shut up, hung, or shot.'

* * *

Gourgaud had many interviews with M. de Stürmer, who reported them word for word to Prince Metternich. He has let me take a copy of what he wrote.

'What did Bonaparte say about the death of Princess Charlotte?'[51]

'He regards it as one more misfortune. Everyone knows that the Princess of Wales has an almost fanatical admiration for him. He hoped that when her daughter came to the throne she would try to have him transferred to England. "Once there," he said, "I am saved." On learning the news he said to me: "Well, there is an unforeseen blow. It is thus that providence plays with all my projects."'

'Does he speak sometimes of his future?'

'He is convinced that he will not stay at St Helena, and continues to believe that the Opposition will prevail.'

'What does he think of the Bourbons?'

'He seems to think that Louis XVIII is a revolutionary and is exposing himself by his conduct to the greatest dangers. "It is not thus," he said, "that dynastic changes are brought about. Prudence ordained that he should distrust all my marshals. He should not have included in his government any element which had not belonged to his party. Labédoyère and Ney[52] were not the only dangerous ones."'

'Does he speak of his wife and his son?'

'He complains of Marie Louise. He thinks she should never have left Paris in 1814. He is convinced that he would still be on the throne if he had married a Russian grand duchess. He speaks often of his son.'

'Do you think he can escape from St Helena?'

'He has had the opportunity ten times, and he still has it at this moment.'

'I confess that that does not seem possible.' 'What is not possible when one has millions at one's disposal? Although I have to complain of the Emperor, I shall never betray him. I repeat, he can escape alone and go to America whenever he wishes. I will say no more about it.'

[He has told this to others; namely, that Bonaparte might escape in a basket of soiled clothes, or in a cask of beer, or a case of sugar; that these means had all been proposed, and considered at Longwood. He has repeated these foolish things to many people, always adding that he would never betray the Emperor. But he has given no further details.]

'If he can, why does he not do it?'

'We have all given him that advice, but he has always rejected our arguments. However unhappy he is here, he secretly enjoys the sense of importance which is evident in his being guarded so closely and the constant interest which all the European Powers take in him. Several times he has told us: "I cannot live as a private personage. I would rather be a prisoner than to be free in the United States."'

'Does he continue to write his history?'

'He works on it intermittently, but my guess is that he will never finish it. When we ask him if he does not want history to depict him such as he really was, he answers that it is often better to let it be guessed than to leave nothing to the imagination. Since he does not believe his destiny to be yet achieved, he does not care to unveil plans the execution of which has not been entirely accomplished, plans which some day he can again take up, with success.'

'Which one of you drew up the observations on Lord Bathurst's speech?'

'The Emperor himself. He dictated most of it to us. It would be better to drop the whole thing there; but you often see in London letters supposed to be written by captains of merchant vessels, which speak a great deal of the Emperor. They are by him. The style is naïve, the details childish, the conception poor.'

'What is his attitude with the people of his suite?'

'That of an absolute monarch. I have often seen him play chess five hours consecutively and keep us standing all that time watching him.'

At Warsaw Bonaparte used to say, 'From the sublime to the ridiculous it is only a step.' At St Helena he repeats a hundred times a day, 'From the Capitol to the Tarpeian Rock it is only a step.' When he is in good humour and likes to chat, which does not often happen, he signs to Bertrand and Montholon to sit near him, and never fails to say, 'Prends un siège, Cinna, prends et sur toute chose . . .'[53] He likes French tragedy, especially Racine's 'Iphigénie,' which he recites rather well; when his humour changes, and he is bored, he walks around the billiard-table, throwing the balls around with his hands, and sings a little Italian air, 'Fra Martino, suona la campana.' Sometimes he has his valet Marchand called, and talks to him of the petty gossip of the town, or else about the details of the kitchen and the household.

I have the honour to be, etc.

No. 9

March 27, 1818.

. . . The Balcombe family has left the island and is going to settle in England. When Bonaparte took leave of Betsy, his favourite, the girl of whom the London papers have spoken so much, he embraced her, cut off a lock of his hair, and gave it to her. Balcombe's departure is much regretted at Longwood. His conduct toward the French was entirely correct, at the same time courteous, and generous.

I have the honour to be, etc.

No. 11

April 10, 1818.

Recently Count Bertrand made me a strange proposal. While talking of Bonaparte's sufferings and misfortunes, he suddenly said: 'The Emperor, bored to distraction, treated inhumanly on this rock, abandoned by the whole world, wants to write his only appeal to the Emperor Alexander. I beg you to transmit this letter.' And he seemed about to take it from his pocket.

'No,' I said, 'it is impossible. It would be failing in my duty.'

'Not at all,' he replied. 'For the Emperor Napoleon would disclose some important revelations to the Emperor Alexander. The point is not so much of aiding an unfortunate man but serving Russia. He will read this letter with pleasure and will be delighted with it. Not to send it to your Court is to neglect your interests, and to sacrifice them to the English. I might remark also that the Emperor paints a picture of you which would make your fortune.'

'I promise,' I told him, 'to report to my Court what you have verbally communicated to me. But I cannot transmit a letter; I have no right; if I did, I should be disavowed.'

'Nonsense,' he cried, 'they might disavow you at St Helena, for form's sake, but in Russia you would be rewarded. Consider the matter further.' Whereupon he left me.

I have the honour to be, etc.

O'Meara's Quarrel with Lowe

No. 13

April 15, 1818.

I have always believed that Dr O'Meara was a spy, an agent of the Governor at Longwood. It was generally believed at St Helena, and the Governor himself has allowed me to think so. But today I am convinced that it is not true. O'Meara has never allowed himself to be so degraded. He gave the English news of Longwood as a matter of interest, just as he gave it to me, a stranger. They have done their best to persuade him to adopt that disgraceful role. But he has conducted himself as an honest man. The Governor has become his enemy, and, by submitting him to the same humiliating conditions, is trying to make him one of the French, which has forced him to resign. O'Meara, however, enjoys the esteem of his Government and has not failed in his duty in any respect. What the Governor is doing to him he would do to any man in the same circumstances—any man who enjoys Bonaparte's esteem. The Governor fears what O'Meara may say of his ridiculous conduct and his indecent attitude toward the Commissioners of the Allied Powers.

> I have the honour to be, etc.

Copy of a Letter from Dr O'Meara to Sir Hudson Lowe

> Longwood, December 23, 1817.

. . . When in August, 1815, Count Bertrand, after having received satisfactory answers from Capt. Maitland of H.M. Ship *Bellerophon* to the enquiries made by him touching my character and conduct, did me the honour to make application to Admiral Lord Keith for me to accompany Napoleon Bonaparte to St Helena in quality of surgeon, his Lordship was pleased to approve of and to sanction my accepting of the above mentioned situation, which, at his Lordship's recommendation, was afterward confirmed by the Lords Commissioners of the Admiralty; the appointment was therefore not of my seeking.

. . . When asked by Napoleon Bonaparte to tell him candidly whether he ought to consider me as surgeon *d'une galère* or as medical man in whom he could repose confidence, I replied that I was not surgeon *d'une galère*; that I was a surgeon and not a spy and one in whom I hoped he might place confidence; that my principles were to forget the conversations I had with my patients on leaving the room, unless as far as regarded my allegiance as a British officer to my Sovereign and country, and that my orders only obliged me to one thing: to wit, to give immediate notice to the Governor in case of any serious illness befalling him, in order that the best medical advice might be promptly afforded.

When minutely interrogated by you, sir, as to the number of interviews and the subject of conversations I have had, and when informed by you, sir, that I was no judge of the importance of the subjects of any conversations I might have, that I had no business to set up my own judgment upon the nature of them, that you might think several things of great importance which I might consider as trifling, I have had the honour to reply that if I was not at liberty to exercise any discretion as to the importance or otherwise of such conversations as I might be present at, there was evidently no other alternative than that of reporting to you every syllable which passed, the doing of which would place me in the situation of a man acting a most dishonourable part; in fact that I would be a spy and a *mouton*, that such conduct would cover my name with well merited infamy and render me unfit for the society of any man of honour.

He who, clothed with the specious garb of the physician, insinuates himself into the confidence of his patient and avails himself of the frequent opportunities and frailties, which his situation necessarily presents, to wring (under pretence of curing or alleviating his infirmities, and in that confidence which has been from times immemorial reposed by the sick in persons professing the healing art) disclosures of his patient's sentiments and opinions for the purpose of afterward betraying them, deserves most justly to be branded with the appellation of *mouton*.

I have had the honour to inform you, sir, that Napoleon Bonaparte, after having satisfied himself of the truth of the assertion that written reports of the state of his health were made by me without his privity, refused, although then very ill, to consult me for several days, and from his well-known character there is no doubt that he would have refused all medical aid whatsoever if his surgeon was obliged to be a spy.

Count Bertrand has signified to me that with respect to the title it might be easy to arrange matters by making use of no proper names in the reports, and by substituting in lieu thereof the word 'personage' or 'the patient'; that provided this was done, previous consent being obtained, and the original deposited with one of the French suite, there would be no objection to written reports of the state of Napoleon Bonaparte's health being made.

. . . It is with infinite pain, sir, that I feel myself obliged to refer to the ignominious treatment which I have suffered from you in your own house, especially upon two occasions. Were I culpable, even a court-martial could not authorize the intemperate and opprobrious epithets so liberally bestowed upon me, being twice turned out of doors in the presence of witnesses, the last time not without some apprehension on my part of experiencing personal violence. I have, sir, had the honour of serving my country in the Royal Navy for several years, until now without censure, and perhaps not without some little commendation, and must protest against any person, however superior to me in rank, making use of language and treatment toward [me] unworthy of and degrading to an officer.

I have, etc.

BARRY O'MEARA,
Surgeon R.N.

Letter from Dr O'Meara to Sir Hudson Lowe

April 12, 1818.

I have had the honour this morning of receiving a letter from Lt.-Colonel Sir Thomas Reade, Deputy Adjutant-General, containing instructions in Y.E. name, by which I find that I am assimilated with the French prisoners at Longwood.

When in 1815 Count Bertrand asked me to accompany Napoleon Bonaparte as surgeon, I declared to Admiral Lord Keith and Captain Maitland that I would accept of the situation on certain conditions; viz., that I should be continued upon the navy list in my rank as surgeon, with my time going on, that it should be permitted me to resign should I find the situation not to be consonant to my wishes, that I should not be considered dependent upon or paid by Napoleon, but as a British officer employed by the British Government, and consequently not subject to any restriction imposed upon French prisoners. The subsequent arrangements made by the Admiralty shew that these conditions were approved of.

In June, 1817, you, sir, manifested some intention of imposing upon me the same restrictions as the French prisoners were subjected to; I had then the honour to communicate to you the stipulations which I had made and the condition; under which I had accepted the situation, adding that I would prefer giving in my resignation to submitting to any such restrictions. I therefore consider, sir, your order of the 10th of this month as a demand for my resignation, and I have the honour, now, sir, to tender it to you, and also to demand permission to return to England.

I have, etc.

BARRY O'MEARA,
Surgeon R.N.

Copy of a Letter from Dr O'Meara to Count Bertrand

April 12, 1818.

. . . It appears clearly to me now that the Governor's intentions, by subjecting me to such restrictions, are to oblige me to quit the chief personage, and I am under the necessity of representing to you, sir, that however painful it is to my feelings to do so in the actual state of ill health in which he is at present, it is impossible for me to sacrifice my character, and my rights as a British subject, to the desire which I have of being useful to him, and I have in consequence formed the resolution to depart and return to my native country. In doing so, I do not conceive that I break through any engagements which I may have contracted with you, since it is caused by a superior power as independent of my will as an irresistible physical force or death itself. It is doubtless true that I made a promise to stay as long as you remained in the state you are, and whilst I would be of any service to you, but in doing so I only expressed my volition, to execute which is now as impossible as if I were labouring under sickness or no more. . . .

I have, etc.
BARRY O'MEARA,
Surgeon.

Letter from Count Bertrand to Sir Hudson Lowe

April 13, 1818.

M. le Gouverneur:

Dr O'Meara informed me yesterday that in consequence of an order from you, he feels constrained to leave the island. I beg you to consider that Mr O'Meara was given us by your Government, on our request, and as a substitute for a French doctor; that he enjoys our confidence; that the Emperor has been ill for seven months with a chronic liver disease, fatal in this country, which is caused by the lack of exercise, which he has not been able to take for two years, and by the way in which you constantly abuse your powers; that things have reached the stage where the patient needs to be cared for every day; that for two years you have wanted to expel Mr O'Meara and to replace him by Mr Baxter; that in spite of your repeated pleas the Emperor has refused to receive that doctor, who inspires him with an invincible repugnance. Consider that if you remove Mr O'Meara, without replacing him by a French or Italian doctor, of known reputation, you will oblige this Prince to die deprived of all help. His agony will be more painful; but the pains of the body are temporary, while the opprobrium which a conduct so inhuman will impress upon the character of your nation will be eternal.

I am charged with stating (1) that Dr O'Meara is the only physician of those on this rock in whom the patient has confidence; (2) that we protest against his expulsion, on whatever pretext it is disguised.

I have the honour to be, etc.

C$^{te.}$ BERTRAND.

No. 17

May 11, 1818.

After the O'Meara affair has been the subject of gossip from one end of the island to the other, the Governor made up his mind, not without much effort and embarrassment, to talk with me about it.

'There is a vessel leaving today for England. Write a report for your Government. But I cannot give you any more bulletins. O'Meara is out, and Baxter is in disgrace with the French. I cannot give you a word about his health. He sees nobody, and I hardly know whether he is even living. What do you think of his illness?'

'They tell me that he is suffering in his head, liver, and stomach, that Montholon spends the entire night at the bedside putting warm cloths on his stomach.'

'Dr O'Meara committed unpardonable mistakes. He kept those people in touch with everything that was happening in the town, in the country, on board vessels. He hunted out news for them and flattered them disgracefully. Moreover, he gave to an Englishman secretly, from Bonaparte, a tobacco-box. What treachery! And is it not shameful that the greatest of all Emperors should try to disregard regulations whenever he possibly can?'

'You don't think, do you, that that is part of a plot, a scheme of escape; or isn't it just a little caprice?'

'Caprice? A hero, a world prodigy, uses just such little tricks as these to corrupt is an abomination.'

'Has Dr O'Meara,' I asked him, 'violated the regulations?'

'No, not exactly.'

'Have you asked him about that, and has he acknowledged it?'

'No, I have not yet asked him directly. I have my reasons.'

'May I speak to you frankly? Tell you my candid opinion, not as Russian Commissioner—for I haven't the right—but as a friend?'

'I shall be greatly obliged to you.'

'If Dr O'Meara is guilty, accuse him and try him publicly, so that in St Helena, Longwood, and Europe they may know what he has done and why you have punished him. But if he is innocent and should be reproached only for peccadillos, forget about the affair and set him at liberty. Remember that if Bonaparte dies without having seen a doctor, as he seems determined on doing, the English will be accused of having poisoned him, and it will be easy for the Bonapartists in France and other places to produce false witnesses against you. And millions of men will henceforth look upon you as his assassin.'

This observation impressed the Governor. He fell into a reverie, then thanked me cordially for my frankness, and left. Two days after this interview Dr O'Meara was set at liberty and restored to full possession of his rights. Bonaparte received him with joy and has already taken a dose of mercury.

I have the honour to be, etc.

No. 20

May 28, 1818.

Since my three years at St Helena are to expire on June 18, 1819, I believe I should profit by such appropriate occasion as presents itself, when that time approaches, to return to Europe, and I cannot fail to inform your Excellency that far from becoming acclimated to this frightful rock, I am constantly suffering from nerves. According to the opinion of all the doctors, the excessive, unbearable heat of the tropics is harmful to my health; and has already weakened it.

I have the honour to be, etc.

* * *

During the winter and spring of this year there was evident some uncertainty among the three commissioners, on account of the lack of sure news of Napoleon's health, as to whether they were wholly fulfilling their duty. If the governor himself was none too sure, their amazement and indignation may be imagined. Occasionally he gives them brief news of a medical nature, but indicates his own lack of trust in it by qualifying it as coming from O'Meara. Having these details 'from Dr O'Meara [June 5], a man under suspicion and devoted to the French, he could not guarantee them. The result is, that since Mr Lowe cannot get along with anyone, and sees treason and traitors lurking everywhere, Europe cannot know what its prisoner is doing.'

* * *

Note from the Governor to the Commissioners of the Allied Powers

June 4, 1818.

I have had the honour to receive your letter of the 24th of May. The declaration contained in the first paragraph of it would have afforded me every satisfaction if I had not been since rendered acquainted with some communications[a] that had been made to you by the followers of Napoleon Bonaparte conceived in a spirit of artifice and design purposely calculated, as I conceive, to mislead and to misrepresent, and although such may not appear to you immediately to affect the security of detention, and that you mention it is your orders to observe and report upon everything, yet I feel persuaded you will admit it is a natural feeling on my part not to suffer any statement from such a source,[b] where it may furnish matter for repetition, to pass wholly unregarded.

If I have been in error in the objections I have shewn to any communication with the followers of Napoleon Bonaparte, when he has himself declined to receive or acknowledge the Commissioners of the Allied Powers, on my offer of presentation to him; and that the conduct of his principal followers and attendants has been at the same time such that it has required the utmost forbearance not to have removed them long since from the Island, the objections are still of such a nature as to remain unabated.

Viewing the communication, notwithstanding, that has ensued,[c] and the inefficacy of the arguments I have offered against it, I feel urged to express to you that as it hitherto has not had my acquiescence, so do I still, under actual circumstances, desire to withhold my assent to it, not being sensible that I therein manifest any objection which is opposed to the due execution of the instructions which you yourself possess.

I beg leave at the same time to express my perfect readiness to present you to Napoleon Bonaparte himself,[d] whenever so required by you, and if he [sic] should arise any obstacle to your personal introduction to him, or that from any motive of your own, you should forbear from urging it, I beg to assure you of my particular desire as well as my readiness to give you every[e] information respecting him whenever you may do me the honour to ask it of me.

I have, etc.

H. Lowe,
Lt. General.

Count Balmain's Marginal Notes

a) He speaks only by conjecture, and brings forth this fact to break through a discussion on the O'Meara affair, which still harasses him. His conscience is not clear, and he wants to know exactly what the Commissioners have learned about it. I stated positively to him that the people of Longwood have made no communication to me which could disturb him in the least, and that is the truth.

b) What I wrote to the Imperial Ministry is verified by a large number of confirmatory documents.

c) I suggested to him to write us officially as follows: 'The Commissioners of the Allied Powers are asked not to pass the enclosure of Longwood and never to speak to the French in any place where they may meet them:' This regulation, I told him, would be clear and positive, and for my part I would scrupulously conform to it. 'No,' he cried, alarmed; 'I could not even think of it. That is not the intention of the English

Government.' 'In that case;' I replied, 'let it no longer be a question of these pretended communications which are only chance meetings and of no importance. You wish me to avoid the French and to turn away when I meet them, and treat them hostilely. Be good enough to indicate it to me in less obscure terms. Take on yourself the blame of a conduct entirely opposed to my instructions, and I shall obey you.'

d) Napoleon has often said that if Marie Louise and his son were to be presented to him by Sir Hudson Lowe, he would not receive them.

e) Where will he get such information? He has only a moral certainty of the existence of his prisoner, and has told me so himself. Nobody at Longwood speaks to him. O'Meara no longer sees him. Capt. Blakeney, orderly officer, has just resigned. He wanted to make him a salaried spy, expecting him to examine bit by bit the clothes, shoes, purchases, dirty linen of the French, and that of course disgusted him. It will be the same with all who take his place.

No. 23

July 11, 1818.

Baron Stürmer has just received his recall. The term of his stay at St Helena, which had been fixed at two years, expired on the eighteenth of last June. He has been named Consul-General in the United States, and sets sail today for Europe. Marquis de Montchenu is charged provisionally, and until it shall please the Court of Vienna to send another Commissioner, with filling his functions and corresponding with the Austrian Ministry.

Not wishing to leave St Helena without seeing Napoleon, M. Stürmer begged Sir H. Lowe to do his best to procure him the occasion, and promised to submit to all the regulations prescribed in similar cases to the simplest tourists. The latter, though not desirous of helping his ambition, went with him to Longwood. But instead of making the customary application to Bertrand, he charged Major Gorrequer with arranging the affair with Montholon. This tactless proceeding angered Napoleon and procured for them the letter of which I send a copy.

Recently, being without news of Longwood, I tried to get some from the Governor. I suspected that he had none himself, but he had written me in his note of June 4, 'I beg to assure you of my particular desire as well as my readiness to give you every information respecting Napoleon Bonaparte whenever you may do me the honour to ask it of me,' and I wanted, by taking him at his word, to see how he would get out of it and to enjoy his embarrassment. He brought me himself his answer, which is nothing but nonsense. Your Excellency will find herewith a copy.

Napoleon is indignant that Austria should have recalled her Commissioner. He has intimated to me through Montholon that he rejoiced at keeping me near him, that I exercised on this rock a controlling influence which, though indirect, was very essential to his safety, that he still hoped from the magnanimity of our August Master that he would never abandon an unhappy Prince, that he adjured him by the memory of old friendship to release him from this frightful exile and to give him another, less unhealthy;—which, being the arbiter of Europe, he could easily do, and generations yet unborn would admire his noble conduct toward a man who had carried fire and sword to the heart of his empire. At the same time he permitted Montholon to give me various curious and interesting notes and documents, among them (1) anecdotes of his marriage with Marie Louise; (2) a story of the battle of Waterloo (the one which General Gourgaud wishes to publish in France is not the correct one); (3) a review of the campaigns of Frederick the Great (Napoleon's hero); (4) the campaign of 1814 and secret details of his return to Paris in 1815.

To collect and copy all these notes I should have to have more time than I dispose of, and also to see the French at Longwood and to receive them at my house.

I cannot close this report without having the honour to inform your Excellency that last month I was seriously ill and that my nerves are still suffering. If the Imperial Ministry judges wise to continue me in this post beyond three years, I should no longer be in a condition to acquit myself of it. The devouring air of this rock is killing me. Even my mind seems weakened.

I have the honour, etc.

P.S. I have just learned that the pamphlet entitled 'Letters Written from the Cape of Good Hope,' which had been attributed to Las Cases, and which your Excellency has no doubt read, is really by Montholon.

Letter from Count Montholon to Sir Hudson Lowe

June 14, 1818.

. . . The Emperor has already attached, and still attaches, considerable importance, if merely from the point of view of health and relaxation, that the principal inhabitants of the island and distinguished travellers should find it possible to cross the barriers of Longwood. It would have been, and would be, useful and pleasant to receive Baron and Baroness Stürmer and Count Balmain as private individuals of distinction, I have had the occasion to discuss this with Baron Stürmer, and he has several times showed me his hope of being thus received. You have prevented this, by making it almost impossible for him to comply with the formalities which are customary on being received at Longwood, which have always been complied with by people admitted there, with not a single exception, *even in your case*.

You could, sir, not expect any favourable result from the proposal which you are now making that the Emperor should receive Baron Stürmer in the presence of an English officer. This application would be importunate and out of place. You would obtain no new reply, since you have known for some time that on that condition he would deprive himself of the happiness of receiving his mother, his wife, or his son.

I have the honour, etc.
Cte. MONTHOLON.

No. 25

July 15, 1818.

... Mr Stokoe[54] surgeon of the Admiral's ship, who had been called to Longwood on the eleventh of this month, has refused to see Napoleon and to consult with O'Meara; the two letters, herewith sent in copy, prove that he is afraid of offending Mr Baxter, the Governor's protégé. ...

I extract the following from the ministerial newspaper, the *Courier*:

> April 27, 1818. The following paragraph relative to Bonaparte is taken from a work just published. As Bonaparte hates Sir H. Lowe, the latter does not unnecessarily trouble him with his presence but delivers all notices to him by Sir Thomas Reade, whose polished manners, good-humoured disposition, and knowledge of the Italian language, which Gen. Bonaparte is said to prefer to French in conversation, makes him a pleasant messenger. Sir Thomas has therefore had more opportunities of becoming acquainted with him in the various affections of his mind than most Englishmen with whom he has conversed.

The whole thing is false. Sir Thomas Reade is the friend, the intimate counsellor, in fact the only confidant, of the Governor, and accordingly communicates with no one at Longwood. He knows a little Italian, but has not studied it; and he is not a 'pleasant,' cultivated man; in other words, a typical John Bull. Napoleon scorns to see him or talk to him, and the English fear him.

Longwood is having printed in Europe two manuscripts both quite interesting. One is entitled 'Manuscrit Venu de l'Ile d'Elbe, par le Comte—' and treats of the events of 1814 and 1815. The other is a second 'Manuscrit Venu de Ste.-Hélène, par le Comte— Auteur du 1er Manuscrit Venu de Ste.-Hélène.' It is an account of the battle of Waterloo.

They are by Napoleon himself. I have just been told so, very confidentially, and I guarantee the fact to your Excellency. The first 'Manuscrit Venu de Ste.-Héléne' is not by him. But he has adopted its ideas, and the second is a supplement.

I have the honour, etc.

No. 27

July 26, 1818.

A great scandal has occurred at Longwood. Lieutenant-Colonel Lyster,[55] who had been offended by Count Bertrand's manners, challenged him to a duel on the twenty-fourth of this month and now threatens him with a beating. He has even insulted Napoleon.

Your Excellency will find enclosed copies of three letters, where the occurrence is related in great detail. I have no time today to add any remarks.

In pursuance to an order from my Lord Bathurst, dated May 16, 1818, communicated yesterday to Dr O'Meara, he has left Longwood this morning forever and is returning to Europe. The same day he received a letter from the Lords of the Admiralty praising his zeal and his conduct and testifying to his capacity, allowing him to expect another appointment, honourable and lucrative. The Governor, on learning that he had kept a diary of Napoleon's illness, directed him positively to leave a copy, or extracts, with Dr Baxter. But he would not part with it. 'Content yourself,' he said, 'with the unofficial bulletins deposited with Bertrand. They are not false or prejudiced. And if you do not believe them, you would not believe my diary.'

I have the honour, etc.

P.S. Dr Verling of the Royal Artillery[56] has replaced O'Meara at Longwood. Napoleon overwhelms Sir H. Lowe with reproaches and insults, is extremely agitated, and does not care to see any doctor. Colonel Lyster has again become Inspector of Militia, and Lieutenant Jackson is named acting Orderly Officer.

M. de Montchenu has asked the King his Master, as reward for his services at St Helena, promotion to the rank of Lieutenant-General, the red ribbon, and an increase of five hundred pounds sterling annually. And from the Emperor Francis twelve hundred pounds sterling, salary as Austrian Commissioner. If he gets all that, we must agree that he has done very well indeed.

Letter from Count Montholon to Sir Hudson Lowe

July 26, 1818.

Yesterday Dr O'Meara left Longwood, forced to abandon his patient in the midst of the treatment which he was directing. This morning that treatment ceased; this morning a great crime began to be committed. The Emperor will never receive any other physician than Dr O'Meara because the latter is his doctor.

I have the honour, etc.

Cte. MONTHOLON.

Reply from Sir Hudson Lowe

July 26, 1818.

. . . I shall not degrade myself or my nation by condescending to reply. . . . If Mr O'Meara's medical attendance was so desirable, he should have combined it with due respect and obedience to the orders and regulations of his Government in other points. The last act of his at Longwood was the breach of an order and the refusal to acknowledge the authority by which it was given.[a]

If Napoleon Bonaparte denies access to any other persons than Count Bertrand and yourself, reflect, sir, on the responsibility which may thus attach to you.[b] I am perfectly prepared to meet any which may fall to my share.

I have, etc.

H. Lowe,
Lt. General.

P.S. I think it right to make known that Mr O'Meara has refused to exhibit his journal of Napoleon Bonaparte's medical treatment, the only document on which any just conception could be formed of his condition or the nature of his complaints or the propriety of the system which may have been adopted for their cure.

H. L.

* * *

Count Balmain's Marginal Notes

a) The day he left Longwood they expressly forbade him to take leave of Napoleon. But he refused to obey this order, and had a long *tête-à-tête* with him in his bedroom.

b) Napoleon had asked that the barriers of Longwood be raised for the principal inhabitants of the island and distinguished strangers. He still desires to admit people to his society. Lord Bathurst has even asked him to draw up a list of fifty people, who might see him freely and without the intervention of the English authorities. But, indirectly, the Governor has interposed opposition, and keeps the French apart, under a thousand false pretexts. I am ready to certify to this and to prove it to all Europe.

Neither O'Meara's departure from the island, nor even the publication of his notorious book, *A Voice from St Helena* (1822), by any means ends his connection with St Helena history or with Hudson Lowe. In a famous lawsuit the latter brought action for libel against the Irishman on the publication of the book. The evidence on the side of Lowe was overwhelming, but his counsel seem to have been criminally careless and negligent in letting the case drag on, until finally the statute of limitations applied and the suit was dropped; nevertheless O'Meara was condemned to pay the costs.

Lowe, says Norwood Young, was made the scapegoat. The government had not the courage to give him the promotion he had so abundantly earned, for fear of arousing further clamour.[57] Bathurst recommended him for the pension which in normal circumstances would have been bestowed, but Lord Liverpool would do nothing for the unlucky man. As no answer to O'Meara's charges was forthcoming, it was supposed that none could be offered, until Forsyth's work was issued in 1853. Once for all this book exposed the worthless nature of O'Meara's statements, but they had enjoyed an unchallenged inning of thirty-one years, and naturally the rejoinder was slow in making its way. Even Lowe's severest opponents now admit that nothing in the '*Voice*' which relates to Lowe is worthy of any notice, unless corroborated by reliable authority. The book is at once one of the most maliciously false and one of the most successful that has ever been published.

A Brazilian Interlude

Balmain's support of O'Meara had estranged him from the governor, and it is evident from now on that a considerable strain is being put upon his nerves. From August to November of this year he spent in a journey to Rio de Janeiro. He was suffering from the 'near view' of local affairs, with no possible distraction. After staring at the same object too long, the sight becomes stony. Sir Hudson Lowe was often attacked, naturally enough, by the same distemper; no man in his position could have escaped it. Balmain had the sense to see that a change would do him good, and when he returned from his holiday he admitted that matters now assumed a different aspect. Reade reported to Lowe that Balmain had said to him that 'since his return from Rio de Janeiro he had quite altered his opinion in regard to the French people at Longwood. He now thought them a 'curious set' [this was his expression], but particularly Count Montholon, whom he described as a very intriguing character.'

At Rio, Balmain was presented to the king[58] by the Russian chargé d'affaires. Perhaps with the recollection of the attempt at escape planned by Colonel Latapie, the king expressed the fear that Napoleon was too near Brazil. Balmain reassured him with a description of Lowe's precautions.

'I have heard,' the King remarked to me, 'that the Governor is not a good man.'

'On the contrary,' I answered, 'he is an excellent man, one who gives himself tremendous trouble for the sake of the tranquillity of both the New and the Old World.'

'Well,' he said, 'I am obliged to him for it.'

'I have been much surprised at the friendliness, and also the extreme timidity, of this monarch.'

The resumption of Balmain's reports was delayed until December 14, since no vessel left the island for six weeks.

* * *

No. 32

December 14, 1818.

. . . A part of Dr O'Meara's correspondence with his London friends was intercepted in October. It arrived at St Helena under the envelop of Mr Forbes, an assumed name, and contained several enclosures, one of which was for Count Bertrand. The Governor alleges that he has uncovered plots, together with intrigues of the party that is working for his recall. The Balcombe family is compromised. When I know more details I shall not fail to communicate them to your Excellency.

The building of the new pavilion of Longwood has been begun. It is a hundred steps from the old, of a regular architecture, and good-looking. Napoleon will have five bedrooms there. I believe it will be completed within eighteen months.

I have the honour, etc.

No. 33

December 20, 1818.

Recently in the course of a conversation with M. de Montholon on the affairs of Longwood, I told him frankly that everything I learned was unfavourable to Napoleon and harmful to his suite. 'I am in considerable doubt,' I said, 'about Dr O'Meara's conduct, especially after the way you have praised it—praise which I repeated many times. I thought him incapable of failing in his duty; yet it is he who is carrying on illegal correspondence.'

'It is a lie, a calumny,' cried M. de Montholon. 'They try to make you believe all that, in order to conceal criminal designs. I give you my word of honour, and am ready to seal it with my blood, that there has been not the slightest plot, nor political correspondence, nor money, sent anywhere. O'Meara has been of no more service to us than to you. What he has done, said, and written is personal to the Governor, aimed at him alone.'

'And this liver disease,' I added, 'this "chronic" and "dangerous" disease, they laugh at it now, as well as your official and unofficial bulletins. Those who have seen the patient at his window or door-step say that he looks very well.'

The whole of this conversation was promptly repeated to Napoleon, who naturally became very angry. He again accused Dr Baxter of drawing up false bulletins, and, recollecting having seen him a few days before at Longwood, he had him forbidden access for good. Perhaps I was wrong in coming out thus against O'Meara, since it has drawn on us a war of correspondence, which apparently will soon figure in the English papers. But it seemed to be my duty, as Russian Commissioner, to point out openly an obvious infraction of the regulations, and especially in M. de Montholon's presence. The Governor quite agrees with me.

I have the honour, etc.

* * *

The 'war of correspondence' centred, naturally, around the 'neglect' of the Emperor's health after O'Meara's departure. Doctors Verling and Baxter were constantly in readiness to give him aid, but the former met with no greater favour than the latter. Montholon returned to the governor a letter from Sir Thomas Reade, because 'the Emperor, as you know, receives no communication unless signed by you.' This letter was in turn sent back because it was written in the name of the 'Emperor.' So the childish and futile exchange continued. Montholon gleefully pointed out Lowe's inconsistency by referring to a number of occasions when the latter had received letters wherein the 'Emperor' was mentioned, and insinuating that letters were returned only when he was unable to answer them and were accepted when he was able to reply.

* * *

Montholon continued:

Sir H. Lowe says he does not know what is meant by 'libellous assertions.' Yet he spreads rumours throughout the island that he has discovered criminal correspondence tending to facilitate Napoleon's escape,[a] and even a political correspondence with Europe.

These two assertions are both libellous. If he had made public what he has intercepted, we should have answered him specifically, but this he has not done. . . .

Count Balmain's Marginal Notes

a) Napoleon is not dreaming of escape now, nor of upsetting Europe. He desires, asks, and hopes only a change of Governor and of exile. That is my opinion.

Count Bertrand has assured me that many Englishmen, out of hatred toward the Governor, had helped, were helping, and would always help Napoleon to communicate secretly with his friends in Europe. It is said that among the letters intercepted at St Helena there was one from Balcombe which ends, 'Those two D . . . Rascals (Sir H. Lowe and his only friend Sir T. Reade) will be soon recalled.' It is certain that there is an important party, both here and in London, which is working to have him recalled. I believe that all the intrigues of Balcombe, O'Meara, etc., have no other object.—Note of Balmain on another observation of Montholon in the same letter.

THE YEAR 1819

No. 1

January 19, 1819.

In the course of a long interview which I had with Sir H. Lowe last month, he tried, in order to prevent me from going to Longwood, to show me that everything done there revolved around myself. 'Bonaparte,' he said, 'believes himself sustained and defended by the Russian Commissioner. That makes him capricious and intractable.' After having vainly tried to prove him wrong, I took the generous decision to help him get what he wanted from me—to break with the French. For an entire month I have seen none, not even at a distance, and learn no news of the prisoner of Europe. When I ask the English authorities they answer always: 'He exists. We know no more.' I was as if incomunicado, seeing only the Governor and his staff, and daring to walk only near Plantation House. Finally I discovered, by pure chance, that there had never been so much argument, intrigue, and gossip at Longwood as during the time when the Russian Commissioner had been invisible. This is a summary of what has happened:

(1) Napoleon, after having promised to live in his new house as soon as he had the keys, declared suddenly that it was badly arranged, improperly located, and uninhabitable.

(2) He had several official notes written to the Governor, very imperious, and forbade the French to sign them. They were all returned to him.

(3) He called upon him imperiously to return to him a family portrait, which, having arrived at St Helena under a false address, had been intercepted last October. This portrait was immediately sent him.

(4) He protested, in insulting terms, against the seizure of the letters from Balcombe, and desired that all this banker's accounts at Longwood should be settled without further delay.

(5) On the night of the sixteenth of this month, having experienced a violent headache and vertigo, he had Mr Stokoe called, who ordered loss

of blood, a hot bath, and a dose of Cheltenham salts. Since then he has become fond of him and is insistent on attaching him to his service. This is not, however, easy to arrange.

Since I seem to have given the Governor a sufficient proof of the small influence which I enjoy at Longwood, I count on returning there within a few days.

I have the honour to be, etc.

* * *

Napoleon's sudden friendship with Stokoe was not to last, for in his next letter, 25 January 25 1819, Balmain reports that he has just heard of the surgeon's recall, 'the Admiral having judged it more prudent to separate him from St Helena.' Stokoe was a great friend of both O'Meara, who had recommended him to the French, and Balcombe.

No. 3

January 30, 1819.

... Here is the second English doctor dismissed from Longwood. With the exception of Baxter, who the French say is a poisoner, Verling, whom they will not see, and Livingstone,[59] who is an accoucheur, there is none other to give them.

Of late Napoleon has had the fantastic idea of making himself a shepherd. He is buying all the fine lambs of the island and likes to pasture them before his window. To keep them from climbing the rocks and getting lost, he has hung a little bell around their necks, and at night shuts them up in a little yard.

Admiral Plampin's squadron, which last year was partially renewed, is now composed of eleven vessels: to wit, the Conqueror (74 guns) [and ten other ships ranging from thirty-four to ten guns].

There is again a great lack of provisions, forage, money, and other necessities at St Helena. It is the seventh or eighth since I have been here and it will not be the last, because Sir Hudson Lowe is not an administrator. He digs trenches, constructs parapets, is always getting ready for a battle, but neglects to build a storehouse.

I have the honour to be, etc.

Napoleon and the Congress of Aix-la-Chapelle

The Congress of Aix-la-Chapelle, in the autumn of 1818, was the first in a continuing series called in the first instance to consider the various revolutions in Spain, Portugal, and Italy, which were making a mock of the Congress of Vienna. Aix-la-Chapelle was followed by Troppau (1820), called to consider the Neapolitan revolt, Laibach (1821), which took steps to suppress that uprising, and Verona (1822), which called in the French army to put down the Spanish revolt.

To Charlemagne's ancient city came Metternich, Richelieu (an invited guest only), Castlereagh and Wellington, Hardenberg, Nesselrode and Capo d'Istria, in order to decide the question of withdrawing the armies of occupation from France, and the nature of the modifications to be introduced, as a consequence, into the relations of the 'Allied' Powers towards each other and towards France. The main outcome was the signature of two instruments—(1) a secret protocol confirming and renewing the Quadrilateral Alliance; (2) a public declaration of the intention of the Powers to maintain their intimate union 'strengthened by the ties of Christian brotherhood,' of which the object was the preservation of peace on the basis of respect for treaties. Many miscellaneous subjects were also discussed which had been left unsettled by the Congress of Vienna or had arisen since, and among them was the treatment of Napoleon. Madame Mère wrote a pathetic letter to the allied sovereigns, and the English Whigs did what they could.

But, despite the hopes which Balmain's reports show to have been placed in the czar by the exiles, Alexander took the leadership in pronouncing against the fallen emperor, and the following protocol (given here, in translation, in the form in which Lowe quotes it to Balmain) was drawn up.

* * *

Protocol No. 42

Separate Article Regarding Napoleon Bonaparte, Aix-la-Chapelle, 21 November 1818

The Russian Plenipotentiaries read a Memoir the purpose of which was to give information on the points of view with which their Cabinet regards the position of Napoleon Bonaparte on the island of St Helena, the spirit of the instructions regulating the conduct of his Britannic Majesty's governor toward this prisoner, and the untruthful reports circulated regarding him by an active malevolence, inspired by a spirit of political prejudice or hostility.

And the Plenipotentiaries of the other Courts, entirely sharing the principles and views of the Russian Cabinet and judging useful to announce explicitly their opinions, both on the facts recorded in the last communications of the British Plenipotentiaries and on the ideas presented with as much truth as force in the said Memoir, have unanimously recognized and declare in consequence:

(1) That Napoleon Bonaparte has placed himself by his conduct outside the pale of the law of nations, and that the measures of precaution taken with regard to him, and all such of that nature as may be authorized, depend entirely upon the discretion and prudence of the Allied Powers.

(2) That the Convention of 2 August 1815, expressly constitutes him a Prisoner of the Powers signatory to the Treaty of 25 March 1815.

(3) That as a result no one among them can be permitted, and still less that Power who is the depository, to depart from the engagement made, or to expose it, by any considerations whatever, to be frustrated, to the detriment of the public peace.

(4) That the precautions ordered in the original Instructions of the Government of his Britannic Majesty and renewed by the despatch of Lord Bathurst to Sir Hudson Lowe of September I, 1818,[a] have obtained the unanimous approval of the Powers signatory to the said Convention, and that they also approve the adjustments [*ménagements*] which humanity and generosity can suggest in the execution of these Instructions, in view of the position in which H.R.H. the Prince Regent now finds himself through the fact that Bonaparte surrendered to the British Government.

(5) That as long as the Commissioners of the Powers which drew up the Treaty of 2 August 1815, prolong their sojourn on the island of St Helena, the Governor of the island will be invited to place them in a full position to fulfil their mission by those means which he may judge most fitting.

(6) That all correspondence with the Prisoner, remission of money, or any communication whatsoever, which shall not have been submitted to the inspection of the British Government, will be regarded without exception as directed against the public safety, and whoever renders himself guilty of such an infraction will be denounced and prosecuted by legal means.

METTERNICH.
RICHELIEU.
CASTLEREAGH.
WELLINGTON.
HARDENBERG.
BERNSTORFF.
NESSELRODE.
CAPO D'ISTRIA.

* * *

a) 'Error of date, the Instruction received by me being dated the 28th Sept. 1818' Signed, H. Lowe.

The receipt of this protocol at St Helena ushers in a new phase in the history of the captivity. It was, of course, received at both Plantation House and Longwood as the final and irrevocable decision of Europe as to the fate of Napoleon. Most of the disturbers—certainly most of those who could be effective—had gone. From December, 1816, to August, 1818, Las Cases, Malcolm, Balcombe, Stürmer, and O'Meara had all left the island; and a time of peace ensued. The drama now marches on, heavily and unrelieved, to its inevitable and not far distant climax. The recurring note of the chorus is supplied by the increasing and always more pessimistic references to the fallen emperor's health.

* * *

No. 4

March 1, 1819.

The last packet from Europe brought us the London papers of July and August. Napoleon, convinced that the Allied Sovereigns, especially the Emperor of Austria, were beginning to take his side against the Governor of St Helena, was awaiting them with extraordinary impatience, and had his suite translate word for word all the articles of the agreement of Aix-la-Chapelle. He was much dissatisfied, for the *Morning Chronicle*, his most zealous defender, hardly speaks of it. The *Courier* crushes him with reproaches and insults. And the *Observer* of August 12 is quite clear that it is our August Master who is handing him over to his destiny. He has again shut himself up in his workroom and sees nobody, so that it is impossible to know what he is doing, and whether he is well or ill.

The extract from my Lord Bathurst's letters, which Sir H. Lowe was ordered to communicate to the French, in reply to their observations on his Lordship's speech of March 18, 1817, is printed in one of these papers and has created a sensation at St Helena. Since the condition of things here is so contrary to that which my Lord Bathurst apparently wishes to establish, everybody is surprised and scandalized. When speaking to the Governor about this extract, I asked him if he expected to obey his instructions and at last to raise the impenetrable barrier of Longwood. He answered, with a little hesitation, that the French had not drawn up the list of people of the island who were to be admitted to their society. The list has been made out since last June, and it is headed by Messrs. Montchenu, de Gors, and myself. He remarked that he himself had presented a list of fifty people and was waiting for it to be approved or rejected. They tell me positively that he has not presented anything of the kind. 'Far from opposing innocent parties and soirées, and distinguished travellers from visiting his prisoner, he has always tried to facilitate them. His conduct toward Admiral Malcolm and the Commissioners of the Allied Powers, who belong to that class and have a right to his confidence, give the lie to that assertion.'

'They tell me,' I said, 'that you have forbidden the officers of the Sixty-sixth to converse with Mme. Bertrand and that they avoid meeting her as much as possible.'

'No,' he cried, 'it is not true, it is a calumny. My officers would not dare to show such conduct, neither toward her husband.'

And since the twenty-sixth he has been worrying me incessantly on these chance meetings. The other day he begged me by all that I held most holy not to see them or speak with them. What can one think of such actions? And what folly to want a thing and yet not to want it at the same time!

Last week, having to settle with Mme. de Montholon an expense account in connection with my trip to Rio, I expressed the desire of calling on her. He thereupon wrote me half a dozen notes and letters, which expose his tortuous policy. I am fully convinced that his reports to my Lord Bathurst are similarly a tissue of subtleties and ambiguities, wherein one can see nothing clearly, judge nothing, or come to any intelligent decision. That is why everything is in confusion here.

I have the honour, etc.

P.S. They have just told me, and the thing is not unlikely, that Napoleon, seeing himself abandoned by the English Ministry and handed over to the sole direction of Sir H. Lowe, wishes to complain of him to Parliament.

No. 5

March 18, 1819.

. . . The French Commissioner has just received a despatch in cipher from the Duc de Richelieu expressly enjoining him to increase as much as possible his relations with Bertrand, Montholon, etc. He has had the kindness to inform me of this. If such an order were sent me, how I should make Mr Lowe dance!

Dr Baxter, to whom his disgrace at Longwood has given a sort of celebrity, has asked and obtained permission to return to Europe. He has been suffering for two years from a liver obstruction and has lost all hope of being cured at St Helena.

I have the honour, etc.

No. 6

March 29, 1819.

The Governor has just informed me that he has received orders (1) to enlarge the enclosure of Longwood as much as possible, so that its bounds would include the entire island outside of the coasts, the bottom of the valleys, and the city of St James; (2) to require positively that Napoleon should be seen by the orderly officer twice a day, morning and evening; and in case of illness, by an English doctor in the service either of the King or the Company, who must moreover be present at all the visits of his private physician and report on them to the authorities. The French have not yet replied to this communication. If the affair is handled tactlessly, as is usual at Plantation House, it will have a bad result.

I have the honour, etc.

No. 7

April 5, 1819.

His Imperial Majesty's frigate *Kamchatka*, Captain Golovin, anchored at St Helena on the first of this month and left on the third. The captain spent two days with me, and the Governor was extraordinarily kind, in great contrast with his treatment of the commander of the other Russian vessel which was here about a year ago. Captain Golovin, famous for his voyages of discovery and his long captivity in Japan, was received here with all honours. The Governor regrets infinitely not having been able to present him to Napoleon, who without doubt would have been charmed to see him and perhaps would have wished to give him a letter for our August Master.

Among the distinguished travellers whom the Company's fleet has brought us this year there is only Mr Ricketts, member of the Council of Calcutta and a near relation of Lord Liverpool, who has seen Napoleon.[60] In order to obtain an audience, he applied, like all his compatriots, to the Grand Marshal, and was presented on the second of this month. Nothing of what happened between them has as yet transpired. The Governor, as well as his staff, are most mysterious about it, and for two weeks I have met nobody at Longwood. Bonaparte received Mr Ricketts in a darkened room. After a quarter of an hour's conversation he had some light brought and said, 'Now I want to see you.' He was in bed, wearing a flannel dressing-gown, with a scarlet turban, was unshaved, and from time to time sat up in bed. The object of this masquerade—for it was hardly anything else—was to touch his visitor by presenting an extremely feeble appearance. I do not know if he is really well or ill. But I am sure that he might have put on trousers, and stood up or sat down, without passing away.

I have the honour, etc.

No. 8

April 12, 1819.

Yesterday I saw Count Montholon and today Count Bertrand. Both spoke of Mr Ricketts's visit to Longwood, and this is in substance what they told me of it. Napoleon charged him with reporting to Lord Liverpool the deplorable and lamentable condition in which he saw him; (2) to beg him, with all the insistence possible, to obtain for Napoleon from the Prince Regent a change of Governor and of exile; (3) to remind him that the wretched inhabitants of Longwood had need of a French or Italian doctor, or even an Englishman who would be their doctor; he asked it on conditions like those imposed on Drs O'Meara and Stokoe; (4) to state to him very clearly that Napoleon would never live in his new house, which they might save themselves the trouble of building. 'I wish,' he cried, 'to die within the four miserable walls and on the miserable cot where for three years they have made me languish pitilessly.' It seems that Mr Ricketts avoided contradicting him and giving any very decided opinions of his own, for Bertrand and Montholon praise him highly and congratulate themselves on having met one honest man among the English.

My Lord Bathurst's new orders have been badly received at Longwood. They deign no reply. They loftily refuse to submit, and for two weeks Napoleon has not shown himself to the orderly officer. The Governor is alarmed and does not know what to do. All indications point to a quarrel.

Mme. De Montholon is dangerously ill with a liver obstruction. Every day they give her ten grains of mercury. Her doctor urges her to return to Europe and assures her that there is no hope of cure at St Helena.

I have the honour, etc.

No. 9

April 22, 1819.

Sir Hudson Lowe, having learned that the Marquis de Montchenu had received orders to enter further into relations with Counts Bertrand and Montholon, has thought best again to protest against any such communications, which according to him are illegal, contrary to the spirit of his regulations; and in that sense he has just sent me two official notes. I have explained on so many occasions the secret motives which actuate him, and furnished so many proofs of the falseness of his statements, that I do not need to say anything further. His real object is to displease the Emperor with me and to have me recalled. He has a perfect mania for writing, and his restless, nervous mind loves to debate and argue, the more trifling the objects the better. If his Imperial Majesty decides to send me a successor, he would be unable to stand all these vexations. My position is no longer bearable. I have been fought for three years without making any trouble or running foul of anybody, but I have no peace or rest, nor any strength left to oppose the ridiculous and unjust pretensions, which are renewed every day.

I have the honour, etc.

* * *

Balmain in a brusque note invites the governor to lodge any complaints of his conduct with the English government. In a footnote to his letter he adds: 'One day, when his mental distress was evidently strong, he said to Montchenu that I was a Bonapartist, and at St Helena it was necessary to be ultra-royalist. My colleagues fell in with this idea and agreed never to see Bertrand, condemned to death by his King, and Montholon, a child of the Revolution. A short time afterward he was ordered to cultivate their society.'

'In order to put an end to this interminable correspondence, and to live at peace with him during the last two months of my stay at St Helena, I have decided to discontinue seeing his prisoners.'

Balmain reports on May 4 that the result of Lowe's fourth note on this subject was to patch up their friendship. So perhaps they served some purpose after all.

* * *

No. 11

May 6, 1819.

Pursuant to his Imperial Majesty's orders, I shall not fail to establish official contact with General Baron de Tuyll, his Envoy at the court of the King of Portugal and Brazil. I am delighted to have nothing disturbing to communicate to him. The activity of the enemies of general peace has not made itself felt on our shores. Bonaparte, as I have already said, demands a change of Governor and of exile, but nothing else. If he is transferred nearer Europe, or to some civilized country, perhaps his ambition will grow. But at St Helena that is all he is aiming at. And I believe that what was determined regarding him at the last meeting of the Sovereigns will cause his hopes to fade. My opinion on the affairs of Longwood is and always will be the same.

I have the honour, etc.

No. 14

June 18, 1819.

I take very great pleasure in being able to announce to your Excellency that my personal relations with the English authorities are peaceful and friendly, that I go continually to Plantation House, where they receive me with open arms, that dinners, balls, and soirées are becoming much more numerous since the arrival of the last news from Europe; and all this detracts from the boredom of my exile. However, it pains me to have to say at the same time that, since I no longer see Bertrand or Montholon, I am completely ignorant of what is happening at Longwood. I have asked the Governor: 'How is Bonaparte; what does he say about the protocol of Aix-la-Chapelle; is he sad, or resigned?' He answers, 'I can only certify to you his mere existence.'

They say in town that consternation reigns among the French, that all they can say is: 'The Emperor Alexander has been deceived by false reports. The English, profiting by the carelessness and apathy of the Austro-French Commissioner and the absence of the Russian, have made the Allied Sovereigns believe what they wish, in order to justify their barbarous conduct. There is absolutely no conspiracy or criminal correspondence.'

It would be my duty to go to Longwood at least twice a month, and they would give me innumerable details regarding all these facts. I know that I am expected there, that they are on the watch for me night and day when out walking, and that Bonaparte, in spite of the decisions taken toward him at the Congress of Aix-la-Chapelle, is still well disposed toward me. But I can do nothing further just now without breaking with Sir H. Lowe.

I have the honour, etc.

No. 15

July 1, 1819.

Today Countess Montholon left for England. Her liver obstruction has apparently become incurable, and the doses of mercury have not dissolved it. She is a woman of heart and head, very charming, and of great use to me at St Helena. My sense of loss is very great. Her husband remains with Bonaparte. Your Excellency will find inclosed a note which Sir H. Lowe has written the Commissioners to acquaint them with Mme. de Montholon's departure. He nowhere mentions her health.

I have the honour, etc.

* * *

Balmain again shows his anxiety to live on good terms with both sides, for, being once more assured by Lowe of his readiness to have him see Napoleon, he answers him, somewhat tartly, on July 25, that he will not fail to give the governor ample notice at any time when he desires to assure himself, with his own eyes, of Napoleon's existence on the island.

* * *

No. 18

August 4, 1819.

. . . On the first of this month the seven to eight hundred Chinese workmen, kept here by the India Company, began a very bloody riot which seems to have been caused by some religious dispute. Formed near Plantation House into three or four bands of about 150 each, armed with bamboo sticks, spears, knives, etc., they rushed upon each other with frightful ferocity. The army of Confucius, uttering piercing cries, gave the alarm to the post at High Knoll. Instead of sending over a strong patrol of dragoons, which would have dispersed them in a moment, they despatched some St Helena sharp-shooters, for the most part drunk, all young lads who were impatient to finish the affair, and who, without waiting for anybody's orders, started shooting wildly. There were some killed and a good many wounded. The commanding officers will be court-martialled.

I have the honour, etc.

No. 20

August 16, 1819.

On the fourteenth, when the orderly officer had as usual approached the Longwood windows, in order to assure himself of Bonaparte's existence, the latter, who had been for some time in his bath, suddenly left it, with tremendous scorn and anger, and showed himself in naturalibus to Capt. Nicholls.

I have no other news to send the Imperial Ministry.

I have the honour, etc.

No. 21

August 25, 1819.

For about two weeks Bonaparte has discontinued his walks, appears no longer at his windows, and shows himself rarely to the orderly officer. The Governor, whom the forty-second protocol of Aix-la-Chapelle seems to have put into a good humour, avoids disturbing him. They know he is at Longwood because they hear him talking and singing; moral certainty is as good as legal evidence. I have just learned that last February, desiring to send to Europe—unknown to the English authorities—a simple letter, he offered six hundred pounds to a captain of a merchant vessel if he would take it. But the latter refused.

The battalion of Island Sharp-shooters, who were tried for murder of the Chinese, have all been declared not guilty.

Surgeon Stokoe has been sent back to St Helena by the Admiralty, to be brought to trial here on ten counts. They are now drawing up the acts of accusation. I shall not fail to keep you posted.

I have the honour, etc.

No. 22

September 2, 1819.

The trial of Surgeon Stokoe took place this morning on board the Admiral's ship by a council of war. After four sessions he was unanimously declared guilty of the accusations brought against him, and was condemned to be dismissed, but, in consideration of his former services, recommended for half-pay. The authorities of the island naturally made a great sensation of this affair and almost persuaded people that he would be hung. He could not get anyone to act as his counsel and had to conduct his own defence, which he did with considerable skill and presence of mind; acknowledged that he had been insubordinate, confessed being the dupe but not the accomplice of the enemies of Plantation House, and moved all who heard him to compassion, so that public opinion today holds him merely a weak, imprudent, and unhappy man. Everyone is wondering why Surgeon O'Meara, who Sir H. Lowe says is much guiltier, is not likewise tried either before an ordinary jury on board the *Conqueror* or before an extraordinary tribunal at London.[61]

No. 24

September 22, 1819.

. . . The transport *Snipe*, leaving England on July 9, arrived at St Helena on September 20. She had on board Messieurs Buonavita and Vignali, priests; Antommarchi, surgeon; Coursot, maître d'hôtel, and Chandelier, cook, all intended for Bonaparte's service. These people, by giving him some news, insignificant as it is, of Europe, have sensibly diminished his boredom for a while. And if Father Buonavita, who has the reputation of being most devout, succeeds in detaching him from the petty concerns of this world, he is the one of the five who will have been the most useful to him. . . .

I have the honour, etc.

* * *

The last sentence in the preceding report was much truer than Balmain could have suspected. It was indeed a strange group of new arrivals who are mentioned in this report. They were all selected by Cardinal Fesch (Napoleon's half-uncle), who lived, always suspected of intriguing for the Bonapartes, under the watchful eye of the Sacred College at Rome. The papal policy decreed that after the original band of followers no Frenchmen should be sent to St Helena; Napoleon was to be isolated to the utmost extent. A case in point is the application for the position of medical attendant from an eminent French doctor, Fourreau de Beauregard. It was declined on the plea that he was not a surgeon.[62] At length Fesch, with the support of Madame Mère, who always espoused the claims of her compatriots, decided upon a young Corsican, Francesco Antommarchi. The amazing thing about him is that he was neither a physician nor a surgeon, but simply an anatomist; he had never practised upon the living. It would have been difficult to find a technically qualified man more unsuited to a post where by this time skill and experience and tact had become so vitally necessary. He had not even the social qualities required, being merely an ignorant provincial from a village in a wild and remote corner of Corsica.

The choice of the two priests is hardly less amazing. Buonavita was also a Corsican, at this time more than sixty-five years old. While acting as chaplain to Pauline Bonaparte at Rome, after Waterloo, he had experienced an attack of apoplexy, which left him a permanent difficulty in his speech. Clearly he needed an assistant. This was provided in Vignali, yet another Corsican, only about twenty-five years of age, who could hardly read and write. Nevertheless, thinking no doubt that it would come in usefully, he had begun a course of medical study. Fesch thought so much of the attainments of this semi-savage that he intended him to act as Napoleon's consulting physician. Says Norwood

Young, 'there is a grim touch in the suggestion. With Vignali as adviser, Antommarchi's qualifications as dissector would soon come into use.'

These three were approved by the church precisely because none of them could speak idiomatic French. With them Napoleon would be tempted to fall back upon the Corsican patois, and he would be encouraged to forget that he had ever been regarded as a Frenchman.

No. 25

October 1, 1819.

Yesterday there was a horse-race at Deadwood. The inhabitants and the garrison were there in large numbers. The Governor and his family also honoured it with their presence. And off to one side I saw Bonaparte's suite, sullen and dejected.

His surgeon Antommarchi has lost no time in making my acquaintance. He is a subtle and clever Corsican, who, I believe, will soon make himself disliked and feared by the English. He assured me that the Emperor Napoleon, his most Illustrious Patient, had an obstruction of the liver, already hard, and that the climate of St Helena would kill him.

Mme. Bertrand tells me that she expects to return to Europe next March; that boredom, melancholy, and nerve trouble had ruined her health. Early every Sunday, she says, Father Buonavita says mass at the Emperor's, and at noon Father Vignali officiates in her rooms. She asked me to attend each of these services regularly.

M. de Montholon who is Bonaparte's emissary to the Commissioners, asked me if I had any news of my successor. 'None,' I answered.

'What,' he cried, 'you don't know that you are replaced? That you are out of favour with your Minister and even with your Sovereign?'

'An invention: believe nothing of it,' I replied brusquely.

'Well,' he said, 'this is what I have been ordered to tell you. "If you see Count Balmain at the Deadwood track,' the Emperor told me this morning, 'tell him from me that his successor was at Paris on the twenty-sixth of last July. That he is a general officer, recommended by his services and good qualities. That this officer, speaking of Count Balmain in Paris society, said positively that his quarrels with the St Helena authorities had caused his recall. That Count Nesselrode, or rather the Cabinet of St Petersburg, disapproved of his conduct, but that the Court was entirely satisfied. That all Europe had recognized in him that unvarying and well-known maxim of the Russians—and of all men of honour—'Generosity and delicacy with a conquered enemy.' Tell him that the Emperor Alexander has continued friendship for me, together with personal sentiments which are and always will be entirely independent of his political attitude. Thank him for the interest which he has taken in my health. I am a captive and so cannot prove my gratitude. Let him not abandon me forever. Try to get along with my assassin."'

Sir Hudson Lowe, to whom I repeated word for word this conversation with Montholon, was immensely surprised and believes it either entirely a figment of the fertile imagination of Longwood, or the beginning of some new intrigue, or an attempt to lay a snare for me. I am not of his opinion.

I have the honour, etc.

No. 26

October 25, 1819.

Since the conclusion of the Congress of Aix-la-Chapelle, the affairs of Longwood have progressed regularly, and, like those of Europe, peacefully. Bonaparte is less unhappy. Occasionally, from temper or grief, he shuts himself up, refuses to show himself to the orderly officer, etc. But, since these caprices no longer seem to disturb anyone, they are disappearing of their own accord. His arguments with Sir Hudson Lowe have entirely ceased. Mme. Bertrand has asked and obtained permission to see more people. Fathers Buonavita and Vignali preach to their flock the virtues of unity, patience, and the practice of good works. They have already married three servants who were living in concubinage. Everything presages the end of intrigues and squalls and the beginning of a state of things at St Helena such as the Allied Powers could entirely approve. Nevertheless I do not dare to answer for the future. It is very possible that this is only the calm before the storm.

I have the honour, etc.

No. 27

November 5, 1819.

. . . The spring equinox has again brought us its toll of dysentery, liver troubles, and inflammatory fevers. The great hospital in town is filled with patients from the Twentieth Regiment. There is no news of Napoleon's health. From time to time he walks up and down before his door, in hunting costume.

I have the honour, etc.

No. 28

November 26, 1819.

The number of sick, especially among the soldiers of the Twentieth, is increasing every day. The average is twenty per company (of sixty men). It is a kind of grippe, which has come upon us suddenly and affects principally the liver or the abdomen. The Admiral has had all the convalescent men of his squadron taken up to a hilltop, where the fresher air contributes to their complete recovery. Captain de Gors has been dangerously ill. I myself have been suffering for five weeks from my liver.

They say that Bonaparte's health is excellent. He has just converted his dining-room into a chapel. Perhaps he will end by becoming devout.

I have the honour, etc.

No. 29

December 1, 1819.

This morning Count Montholon told Sir Hudson Lowe that Napoleon's health was becoming better every day and that he might decide to ride horseback. For some days he has been amusing himself with gardening and puts his whole suite hard at work—men, women, even old Father Buonavita.

Lord Charles Somerset, Governor of the Cape of Good Hope, is expected at St Helena toward the end of this month. He is en route to London, on leave.

I have the honour, etc.

THE YEAR 1820

No. 1

January 10, 1820.

I have nothing new or interesting to communicate to the Imperial Ministry. Bonaparte's affairs are always the same. He leads a tranquil life, seems to enjoy good health, and is extremely busy with his garden. He is having big trees placed, and flowers planted, which he waters himself, in full view of every one. This morning the orderly officer wrote to Plantation House as follows:

I saw General Bonaparte this morning. He was amusing himself in one of his private flower gardens. His morning dress at present consists of a white gown, and straw hat with a very wide brim. In the afternoon he appears out in a cocked hat, green coat, and white breeches and stockings. He walks a good part of the afternoon in Longwood garden, accompanied by either Counts Montholon or Bertrand, and often pays a visit to the Bertrands in the evenings. Yesterday afternoon he walked around in the new garden and buildings.

G. NICHOLLS.

Pursuant to an order from my Lord Bathurst, Sir H. Lowe has enlarged the second precincts of Longwood. He has added, toward Plantation House, a very pleasant promenade of seven or eight miles, and has just addressed to the Commissioners, in order to inform them of this new arrangement, the memorandum which your Excellency will find enclosed.

The fever and other inflammatory diseases continue to make great inroads among the garrison.

I have the honour, etc.

No. 2

January 28, 1820.

On the seventeenth I met Count and Countess Bertrand driving in a four-horse open carriage. They remarked, as we passed, that Bonaparte's health was good, that he was devoting himself entirely to gardening, and that he was quite satisfied with the present conduct of Sir Hudson Lowe. For four or five days he has been amusing himself with shooting chickens and other animals which enter his garden. Yesterday he killed Mme. Bertrand's favourite goat, believing it to belong to the orderly officer.

Lord Charles Somerset, Governor of the Cape of Good Hope, arrived on the twenty-fifth. He applied to M. de Montholon for an audience with Bonaparte but received no reply whatever. This morning his Lordship sailed away in very bad temper.

I have the honour, etc.

No. 3

February 10, 1820.

Bonaparte enjoys the best of health. He is in very good humour and works hard in his garden. I have copied two reports of the orderly officer, dated February 6 and 8:

General Bonaparte has been amusing himself this morning in shooting fowls: I understand he fired five shots, and killed three hens, one of which belonged to Novaray (his Swiss), who appeared much offended at having his fowls thus disposed of, particularly as this was not the first time they had suffered from the effects of the General's fowling-piece. I believe the fowls intrude rather too much in the General's favourite flower garden.

A few minutes after the Governor left Longwood this afternoon I saw General Bonaparte. He was crossing the garden to pay a visit to Count Bertrand. The General was accompanied by Count Montholon.

At the beginning of summer I had expected to resume my trips to Longwood in order to be entirely sure of what was happening. But I have been ill for about three months. I am much weakened and hardly go out of the town.

I have the honour, etc.

No. 4

February 18, 1820.

Blood is flowing at Longwood. Bonaparte has just bought a flock of goats and is doing considerable execution. It amuses him to fire on them one after another. Today it is his favourite sport. For the rest, he is at peace with the English, and his health is excellent. The French attribute his recovery, almost miraculous, to the great skill of the surgeon Antommarchi.

I have the honour, etc.

No. 5

February 27, 1820.

The cholera morbus is making terrible ravages at present at the Ile de France.[63] Already many have died of it at the Cape of Good Hope and some at St Helena. The approach of this plague greatly upsets Sir Hudson Lowe. In order to preserve our little colony from its ravages he has submitted all vessels coming from India to the inspection of Mr Arnott,[64] Surgeon of the Twentieth Regiment, and in addition has just published some sanitary regulations a printed copy of which Your Excellency will find enclosed.[65]

I have the honour, etc.

No. 7

March 10, 1820.

On the seventh of this month I received the letter which your Excellency did me the honour to address me on September 12, 1819. In conformity with the gracious and kindly order of our August Master, his Majesty the Emperor, I shall leave as soon as it is practicable my sad and stormy post at St Helena, to proceed to St Petersburg. Those vessels of the East India Company which were not already loaded with troops or with sick have already gone by. However, five or six are expected toward the middle of the season, among them the *Bombay*, the *Hertfordshire*, the *William Pitt*, with whose Captains I am well acquainted, and which offer a comfortable passage. The moment of my departure will depend entirely on that of their arrival. Up to then I shall continue to send reports to the Imperial Ministry.

This morning the orderly officer wrote to Plantation House as follows:

About six o'clock yesterday evening General Bonaparte undressed and plunged into the stone reservoir in the garden. Count Montholon was with him, and two servants attended to dry and assist the General in dressing. I saw him for some time in the garden this morning.

E. LUTYENS,
Capt. 20th Regt.

I have the honour, etc.

No. 8

April 18, 1820.

All is perfectly tranquil and in good order at St Helena. Bonaparte takes considerable exercise in his garden. His complexion is fresh and healthy, his air pleasant; in other words, quite another man. Count Montholon and Mme. Bertrand assure me that he is still having some trouble with his chronic disease, hepatitis, and often takes mercury, but that, thanks to the assiduous care of M. Antommarchi, it is no longer dangerous. Your Excellency will find enclosed three reports of the orderly officer.

Since March 13 twenty vessels of the India Company have anchored at St Helena, all fully loaded both with passengers and merchandise. The Captains, anxious as they were to be of service to me, could only offer me a hammock in the common room. Dr Verling, who like myself is under orders to return to Europe, has remained here for the same reason. Two very large vessels, coming from China, are hourly expected. On one of them we hope, and are almost sure, to find comfortable quarters.

I have the honour, etc.

Longwood, April 5th.

General Bonaparte remained out until two o'clock yesterday and finished the sod wall. The four Chinese, who have been constantly employed in the garden, got angry at the General having given a bottle of wine to each of the Chinese that are employed in the house and did not give them the same indulgence. They therefore refused doing what the General wanted them to do, which put him in a great rage, and he ordered them off instantly.

General Bonaparte is hard at work this morning in the same garden. He has cut a large hole like an embrasure in the sod wall facing my side window, in which they are now fixing a large tub, half up the wall, to form a sort of cascade into the long tank in the garden. The General is accompanied by Count Bertrand. Count Montholon was not out the whole of yesterday. I have not seen or heard of him this morning.

April 13

General Bonaparte was out with Count Montholon the whole of yesterday evening. He has been at work the whole of this morning, with Counts Bertrand and Montholon.

April 16

About seven o'clock last night General Bonaparte was walking in the gardens with Count Montholon, when he discovered some cattle belonging to the farm in the outer garden. He immediately ordered his two fowling-pieces to be brought, loaded with ball, both of which he fired, and killed one of the oxen. I believe there is another slightly wounded in the leg.

Count Montholon mentioned to me that he saw the cattle come in at the outer garden gate. The gates are the only way the cattle could enter, the fence being perfectly secure; and the gate must have been left open by some of the establishment, for they never think of closing them when they pass in or out. Count Montholon said the General was determined to adopt the same plan if he again saw the cattle in the garden. I told him that it was very dangerous firing ball in the garden, and that General Bonaparte might have killed one of the sentries; upon which he said the General took the precaution of going round, and firing toward the house. Which must have been the case, from the way the animal was wounded   and fell. It lays upon its right side, at the foot of the little mound that is surrounded with a myrtle hedge.

E. LUTYENS,
Capt. 20th Regt.

P.S. This animal is a grievous loss at St Helena. The employees of the India Company are much incensed and distressed. Anyone other than Bonaparte after such a deed would be hailed before the King's Bench.[66] I had a Newfoundland dog which for having killed a sheep was condemned to death by the Magistrate at St James and executed.

* * *

In March Count Balmain was married to Charlotte Johnson, Lowe's elder stepdaughter, and on May 3 they left St Helena in the *General Harris*.

APPENDIX

Sir Hudson Lowe K.C.B., G.C.M.G., 1769–1844.
Lt-General, Governor of St Helena

Hudson Lowe was from a Lincolnshire family long settled near Grantham, but he was born on 28 July 1769 in Galway where his father, also named Hudson Lowe, was stationed with the 50th foot, as surgeon and afterwards, as staff surgeon-major. The family went to Jamaica in late 1772. After nearly four years the 50th moved to North America, where most of the men were dispersed to other regiments. However, in November 1776 Lowe's father returned to England with a recruiting party to Salisbury, and the younger Hudson attended school there. In 1778 when the family were at Plymouth Hudson Lowe junior became an ensign in the East Devon militia, passing review with it before the age of twelve. The 50th moved to Gibraltar in 1784, where Lowe junior served as a volunteer in 1785–6, and was gazetted ensign on 25 September 1787, advancing to lieutenant in the regiment on 16 November 1791, and captain-lieutenant and captain on 6 September 1795. Meanwhile, he had travelled on leave through Italy, picking up an intimate knowledge of Italian and French. On the outbreak of war he rejoined his regiment at Gibraltar and served with it at Toulon (1793) and at the capture of Corsica (1794), taking part in the attack on the great Martello tower, the storming of the Convention redoubt, and the sieges of Bastia and Calvi. He remained two years in garrison at Ajaccio, then went with the 50th to Elba, where he was deputy judge-advocate. Subsequently he was stationed in Portugal for two years and became proficient in Portuguese, having already obtained a good knowledge of Spanish. From Lisbon he moved in 1799 to Minorca, where he was made one of the inspectors of foreign corps and put at the head of 200 anti-republican Corsicans—styled the Corsican rangers—with the rank of major-commandant from 5 July 1800. He commanded the corps in Egypt in 1801 at the landing and in the operations before Alexandria and the advance on Cairo. In 1803, on the recommendation of Moore, Lowe was appointed one of the new permanent assistants in the quartermaster-general's department and was stationed at Plymouth, from where, in

July, he was dispatched to Portugal to inspect the troops and defences on the north and north-eastern frontiers; and he reported the feasibility of defending the country with a mixed British and Portuguese force. He was then sent to Malta to raise a new and larger corps of foreign men, to be called the Royal Corsican rangers, as major-commandant from 15 October 1803 and lieutenant-colonel-commandant from 25 June 1804. Following a mission to Sardinia, in 1805 Lowe went with his corps to Naples. When the British retired to Sicily he was detached with part of his corps, the rest joining him, after the battle of Maida in July 1806, at Capri, where he was reinforced later by the Malta regiment. Lowe occupied Capri from 11 June 1806 until 20 October 1808, when, after thirteen days' siege—the Malta regiment having been made prisoners and the defences of Capri breached—he surrendered to a French force under General Count Jean-Maximin Lamarque. He blamed the disaster on the absence of naval aid and the conduct of the Malta regiment.

Lowe commanded the Royal Corsican rangers in the expedition to the Bay of Naples in 1809 and distinguished himself at the capture of Ischia. He then acted as second in command of the expedition to the Ionian Islands (1809–10). Lowe was put in command of the left division of the troops in the Ionian Islands and entrusted with the provisional government of Cephalonia, Ithaca, and Santa Maura, which he administered for two years. He was promoted colonel-commandant of the Royal Corsican rangers on 1 January 1812 and retained that post until the corps was disbanded at the beginning of 1817.

In January 1813 Lowe was sent to inspect the Russian German Legion— a force composed of German fugitives from the Moscow retreat—which was to be paid by Britain. He remained with the Russian army for the ensuing campaign, being present at the battles of Bautzen and Würschen. During the short-lived armistice of June to July 1813 he inspected some 20,000 levies in British pay and joined Major-General Sir Charles Stewart at the headquarters of Crown Prince Bernadotte of Sweden. Stewart sent Lowe to the headquarters of the Prussian army of Silesia under Marshal Blücher, with whom he was present at Möckern, at the great battles around Leipzig, and at the pursuit of the French to the Rhine. He then resumed his inspections in north Germany and at the end of the year was ordered to organize a new body of Dutch levies in the Netherlands. This plan was abandoned, apparently at his own request, and on 24 January 1814 he rejoined Blücher at Vaucouleurs. As the only British officer of rank with Blücher's army, Lowe was privy to many important deliberations, especially during the conferences at Châtillon, where he strongly advocated the advance on Paris. He was the first officer to bring to England the news of Napoleon's abdication, arriving in London on 9 April 1814, after having ridden from Paris to Calais through potentially hostile country attended by a single cossack.

Lowe was knighted on 26 April 1814 and promoted major-general on 4 June. When the allies withdrew from France, he became quartermaster-general of the army in the Low Countries under the command of William Frederick, prince of Orange. The Duke of Wellington assumed command in the Netherlands early in April 1815, and Lowe remained for a few weeks under him as his quartermaster-general, but he was condemned by the duke as a 'damned old fool' for hesitant map-reading and was replaced in May by Colonel Sir William Howe de Lancey. The day after the battle of Waterloo, Lowe took command at Genoa of troops gathered to co-operate with Austro-Sardinian forces. In July, in conjunction with a naval squadron under Admiral Sir Edward Pellew, he occupied Marseilles, and then marched against Toulon, where, in concert with the royalists, he drove out the Napoleonic garrison.

At Marseilles, on 1 August 1815, Lowe received the news that he would have the custody of Napoleon. St Helena was a possession of the East India Company, and on 23 August the court of directors notified him that they had appointed him governor with a salary of £12,000 a year, undoubtedly at the behest of the Government which had temporarily taken control of the island. No stipulation was made as to pension, which explains why his critics could later claim that he was not considered eligible for pension. On 12 September he received from Bathurst, secretary of state for war and the colonies, preliminary instructions about dealing with Napoleon. He obtained the local rank of lieutenant-general on 9 November, and on 4 January 1816 he was made KCB. Sir Hudson and Lady Lowe accompanied by one daughter left for St Helena in the *Phaeton* frigate, 29 January 1816, and arrived 14 April 1816.

Lowe had just six meetings with Napoleon during the whole of the five years they co-inhabited the island. First visit, 17 April 1816. Second visit, 30 April 1816. Third visit, 17 May 1816. Fourth visit, 20 June 1816. Fifth visit, 16 or 17 July 1816. Sixth visit, 18 August 1816. Lowe saw Napoleon by accident on 4 August 1819, and again about 20 November 1820. Lowe was unable to establish any satisfactory relationship with Napoleon. Supposedly at their first meeting, when the governor addressed him as 'General Buonaparte', Napoleon observed: 'His eye is that of a hyena caught in a trap' and his dislike intensified, as Lowe insisted on still-tighter security. Lowe and Napoleon met six times in just four months and then no more. The last two formal meetings were particularly acrimonious; though Lowe maintained self-control in the face of considerable verbal abuse. After 18 August 1816 he refused to make further visits to Longwood, though a contrary version holds that Napoleon declined to see Lowe again because 'he makes me too angry and I lose my dignity'. He also told Charles Ricketts, a nephew of the prime minister, Lord Liverpool, that Lowe 'was one of the few men that your uncle should never have sent here', due to his association with 'the Corsican battalion', which Napoleon considered a collection of renegades and deserters. Indeed, views similar to Napoleon's were independently expressed. Wellington thought Lowe 'a very bad choice ... wanting in education and judgement ... a stupid man ... [who] was suspicious and jealous'. Count Balmain declared him 'not a tyrant, but he is troublesome and unreasonable beyond endurance'. Officers who were on the spot all the time, and were personal friends of various members of Napoleon's staff, pointed to the real origin of many criticisms of Sir Hudson Lowe that have found general acceptance. Walter Henry, assistant surgeon in the 66th foot, which formed part of the St Helena garrison from 1816 to 1821, became convinced that Lowe's vigilance and his firmness in suppressing plots at Longwood were the cause of the hostility towards him, rather than any want of temper or courtesy. Lieutenant Basil Jackson, a Royal Staff Corps officer at St Helena, after noting reliance placed by the exiles on party sympathy in England, concluded:

> The policy of Longwood—heartily and assiduously carried out by Napoleon's adherents, who liked banishment as little as the great man himself—was to pour into England pamphlets and letters complaining of unnecessary restrictions, insults from the governor, scarcity of provisions, miserable accommodation, insalubrity of climate, and a host of other grievances, but chiefly levelled at the governor as the head and front of all that was amiss.

On 12 April 1816 a warrant had been issued, addressed to Lowe as 'lieutenant-general of his Majesty's army in St Helena and governor of that island', requiring him to detain and keep Napoleon as a prisoner of war, under such directions as should be issued from time to time by one of the principal secretaries of state. In fact the attitudes of certain members of the British Government were verging on the paranoid in their fear of Napoleon escaping the island as evinced by the large military and naval forces maintained on and around the island. Lowe, it seems, took all of the instructions absolutely literally and felt that he had no room for manoeuvre. He therefore, felt compelled to restrict Napoleon's freedom of movement. This restriction, bad enough as it was, became further compounded by pettiness. The insistence on referring to Napoleon as 'General', and the confiscation of any book or item that held the Imperial inscription displayed lack of tact and were possibly the 'pricks to pride' that rubbed salt into the wound of containment.

Lowe did, however, do some positive things which should be mentioned. Shortly after his arrival, he realised that the funds for running Longwood were insufficient and raised the annual allowance from £8,000 to £12,000. In 1818 he abolished slavery on the island, without compensation, which took effect from Christmas day 1818, although exactly how slaves were to leave the island without funds for transportation remains a question which was never answered.

Napoleon died on 5 May 1821. At the end of July Lowe handed over the governorship to Brigadier-General John Pine Coffin and left St Helena on 25 July 1821, in the *Dunira*. Back in England, Lowe was cordially received by George IV; and on 4 June 1822, he was appointed colonel of the 93rd foot, the Sutherland Highlanders.

In August 1822 Barry Edward O'Meara, who had been Napoleon's doctor at St Helena, published in London his highly critical *Napoleon in Exile: a Voice from St. Helena*. O'Meara had resigned as Napoleon's doctor complaining of restraints placed on him by Lowe and had been ordered off the island in July 1818. On 2 November 1818 O'Meara had seen his name removed from the navy list for defamatory allegations about Lowe. The book was a huge success and went through five editions in a few months. The glaring inconsistencies between some of its statements and others previously made by O'Meara were exposed in the October 1822 issue of the *Quarterly Review*; nevertheless, this had not stopped the book's huge success. Lowe sought legal redress, and a rule *nisi* for a criminal information against O'Meara was obtained in Hilary term 1823 but was afterwards discharged on a technical objection in respect of time. Lowe was then advised that he had done everything necessary by denying the various charges on affidavit, as O'Meara, if he challenged the truth of the denials, could proceed against him for perjury. He was, therefore, dissuaded from further proceedings against O'Meara, though he was strongly advised by Lord Bathurst to publish a full and complete vindication of his governorship of St Helena from the materials in his possession. He appears, however, to have thought that the government was bound to defend his character as a public servant, whose conduct it had approved.

In 1823 Lowe was appointed governor of Antigua but quickly resigned for domestic reasons. He was then appointed to the staff in Ceylon as second in command under Lieutenant-General Sir Edward Barnes. He left his family in Paris and late in 1825 set out for Ceylon, where he remained until 1828, at which time implied criticisms in the last volume of Sir Walter Scott's *Life of Napoleon* brought him home on leave. He met with a hearty welcome at St Helena on the way, but his return was not well received in official quarters because the reasons for it were deemed inadequate.

Appeals to Bathurst and also to Wellington, who advised him to go back to Ceylon and look forward to succeed to the chief command, proved fruitless. His promotion to lieutenant-general on 22 July 1830 virtually coincided with the opposition party coming to power. Ceylon received a new governor, and Lowe's hopes of further preferment or pension were never fulfilled. He returned to England in 1831 and from that time until his death in 1844 incessantly pressed the government in respect of his claims.

Lowe died at Charlotte Cottage, near Sloane Street, Chelsea, London, of paralysis on 10 January 1844, aged seventy-four. His papers were entrusted to Sir Harris Nicolas to prepare for publication, but the arrangement was abandoned after many delays. Subsequently, they were placed by the publisher of the *Quarterly Review* in the hands of William Forsyth, who compiled the *Captivity of Napoleon at St Helena, from the Letters and Journals of Sir Hudson Lowe*, 3 vols., 1853.

For further detail on Hudson Lowe see the full article in the *Dictionary of National Biography*.

ENDNOTES

These notes are a combination of Julian Park's original notes, substantially expanded for the 2014 edition. All books and articles mentioned are entries by Park and refer to publications prior to 1928.

1. *Reflections on the Napoleonic Legend*. New York, 1924.
2. *Les Origines de la Légende Napoléonienne*. Paris, 1906.
3. *Napoleon in Exile: St Helena*. 2 volumes. London, 1915.
4. M. A. Aldanov: *Saint Helena, Little Island*. New York, 1924. This little book is written around Balmain, and, although he is treated somewhat fancifully, it has been able to include a number of interesting personal details, through the collaboration of Count J. A. de Balmain, the commissioner's descendant. Curiously enough, Aldanov confuses Lady Lowe's two daughters and has Balmain marry Susanna instead of Charlotte.
5. According to de Gors, the marriage distressed Napoleon terribly.
6. These words were underlined by the Czar.
7. Secretary of state for foreign affairs, 1816–56. As the czar veered toward Metternich's system Nesselrode became more and more his mouthpiece.
8. The two dates reflect that Russia remained on the Julian Calendar, and did so until 1917. Therefore, 18 December was the Julian date and 30 December was the Gregorian date.
9. Ukase—an edict of the czar.
10. Major-General Beatson was governor of the island from 1808 to 1813. The East India Company had taken possession of it, after the Dutch left, in 1651; and although the form of the name as given in these reports varies, the capital was called Jamestown, in honour of the Duke of York, afterward James II. In 1813 Colonel Mark Wilks succeeded Beatson as governor and remained there until the arrival of Sir Hudson Lowe in April, 1816. The population of the island, just before Napoleon's arrival, was 1,871 (exclusive of the small garrison), of whom only 776 were white. The island was given up to the crown during the residence of Napoleon, the Company agreeing to pay to the crown an annual sum based

upon the average cost of administering the island during the three preceding years. On Napoleon's death and Lowe's departure, it reverted to the Company, and did not definitely become a crown colony until 1836. At the present day [1928] the population is hardly larger than a hundred years ago, and the whites number only 250. *Editor note:* the population in 2014 is approximately 4,250.

11. Sir George Cockburn, eighth baronet, (1772–1853). Cockburn joined the Royal Navy in 1786 and by 1814 had risen to the rank of Rear Admiral. In August 1814, Cockburn accompanied the joint naval and military force under Major-General Ross, which after the battle of Bladensburg seized the city of Washington for twenty-four hours. Cockburn also accompanied Ross in the subsequent advance against Baltimore, and was with him in the skirmish on 12 September in which Ross was mortally wounded. Between January and March 1815, while Cochrane attempted to take New Orleans, Cockburn undertook diversionary attacks on the coast of Georgia from a base on Cumberland Island. He was recalled to England following the conclusion of peace, only to find, on anchoring at Spithead on 4 May, that war with France had again broken out. He was ordered to hoist his flag on board HMS *Northumberland* and to convey Napoleon to St Helena, which he reached on 15 October. He remained there as governor of the island and commander-in-chief of the Cape of Good Hope station until the summer of 1816, when he was relieved by Sir Hudson Lowe and Sir Pulteney Malcolm. He was a junior lord of the Admiralty between April 1818 and May 1827, a member of the council of the lord high admiral between May 1827 and September 1828, and then first naval lord until November 1830.

Cockburn, of course, was a sailor and not a diplomat or politician, and apparently did not know how to conduct himself in the presence of either Napoleon or his followers. Las Cases in his journal gives a long list of the "insults" they had received from Cockburn, but there was, says Norwood Young, no justification for any of these complaints any more than for the subsequent similar clamours against Lowe. The French policy for the present was to denounce Cockburn, and part of the reason for that policy was a childish attempt thereby to curry favour with the new governor, Lowe, with whom, for a few weeks, relations promised to be most cordial. When Las Cases remarked that he was afraid the new governor would think they were intractable, "we who are by nature so gentle and patient, the Emperor could not prevent himself from smiling and pinching my ear."

12. Sir Pulteney Malcolm, (1768–1838). Sir Pulteney entered the Royal Navy as a midshipman in 1778 and had a distinguished career. At the end of the war Sir Pulteney was appointed commander-in-chief of the St Helena station and succeeded Sir George Cockburn. He arrived in HMS *Newcastle* on 17 June 1816. He conducted himself with such firmness and gentleness combined, and so greatly to the satisfaction of Napoleon that the latter, while he discharged the whole brunt of his indignation upon the unlucky head of Sir Hudson Lowe, had an entirely different feeling for the admiral. "Ah! there is a man," he exclaimed, "with a countenance really pleasing: open, frank, and sincere. There is the face

of an Englishman—his countenance bespeaks his heart; and I am sure he is a good man. I never yet beheld a man of whom I so immediately formed a good opinion as of that fine soldier-like old man. He carries his head erect, and speaks out openly and boldly what he thinks, without being afraid to look you in the face at the time. His physiognomy would make every person desirous of a further acquaintance, and render the most suspicious confident in him." Such was the striking portrait of Sir Pulteney drawn by the hand of a master—one who was the greatest of painters through the medium of language, as well as the first of epic poets by deed and action. On one occasion, when the impatient spirit of the exile burst forth, he exclaimed to the admiral, "Does your government mean to detain me upon this rock until my death's-day?" "Such, I apprehend, is their purpose," replied Sir Pulteney, calmly. "Then the term of my life will soon arrive," cried the indignant ex-sovereign. "I hope not, Sir," was the admiral's answer, "I hope you will survive to record your great actions, which are so numerous, and the task will insure you a term of long life." Napoleon bowed at this gratifying and well-merited compliment, and quickly resumed his good humour. Sir Pulteney continued in the command of the St Helena station from June 1816 to June 1817; and when he left it he was on the best terms with Napoleon, who frequently afterwards used to speak of the pleasure he had enjoyed in his society. Sir Pulteney married, 1809, Clementina, daughter of William Fullerton Elphinstone.

13. Rear-Admiral Malcolm's handsome presence and engaging manners soon won him Napoleon's warm regard, and with Lady Malcolm he paid the emperor many visits at Longwood. Although Malcolm did all he could to smooth over the differences between Lowe and Napoleon, his close relations with the emperor were viewed with suspicion by the governor. No open rupture took place, but at the expiration of his command, in June, 1817, Malcolm left the island with no very friendly feeling toward Lowe. Lady Malcolm, Mrs Skelton, and Mrs Balcombe were the only English ladies who were at all intimate with Napoleon.

14. This episode is of course always cited as an outstanding example of Lowe's tactlessness. Cockburn had invited Napoleon to dinner by word of mouth, at which informality the Emperor had taken offence. Lowe therefore imagined, correctly enough, that Napoleon must be addressed in writing, but should have known enough of the character of his prisoner and of the necessity for consistency on the latter's part not to have addressed a social letter to him as 'General.' That form might have done in official communications, to which no reply was necessary, but its use in this way illustrates the greatest defect in the psychology of Hudson Lowe.

Lady London and Moira, wife of the governor-general of India, was a guest at Plantation House. A day or two after this episode Napoleon willingly received some of her friends who were traveling with her.

15. 'Lady Lowe was a woman of attractive appearance, and lively and agreeable manners.'—Norwood Young.

A letter in *The Times* of 26 November 1842, signed by 'An Old Inhabitant of St Helena,' says that 'the inhabitants generally remember with the liveliest feelings of affection the charities and benevolence of Lady Lowe.'

16. Charles Tristan, Marquis de Montholon, (1782–1853). Entering the army in 1797, Montholon rose with rapidity and avowed himself, when chef d'escadron in Paris at the time of the coup d'état of November 1799, entirely devoted to Napoleon. He served at the Battle of Jena and distinguishing himself at the battle of Aspern-Essling where he was wounded. At the end of that campaign on the Danube he received the title of count and remained in close attendance on Napoleon, who confided to him several important duties. He was chosen for a mission to discuss diplomatic matters with the Austrian commander Archduke Ferdinand Karl Joseph of Austria-Este at Würzburg among others. At the time of the first abdication of Napoleon at Fontainebleau, Montholon was one of the few generals who advocated one more attempt to rally the French troops for the overthrow of the allies. In exile with Napoleon after the second abdication he, with his wife, Albine de Montholon, accompanied the emperor to Rochefort, where Napoleon and his friends finally adopted the proposal, which emanated from Count Las Cases, that he should throw himself on the generosity of the British nation and surrender to HMS *Bellerophon*. Montholon and his wife accompanied the ex-emperor to St Helena. Napoleon chiefly dictated to Montholon the notes on his career which form so interesting, though far from trustworthy, a commentary on the events of the first part of his life. Montholon is known to have despised and flouted Las Cases, though in later writings he affected to laud his services to Napoleon. With Gourgaud, who was no less vain and sensitive than himself, there was a standing feud which would have led to a duel but for the express prohibition of Napoleon. Las Cases left the island in November 1816, and Gourgaud in January 1818; but Montholon, despite the departure of his wife, stayed on at Longwood to the end of the emperor's life. Those who believe that Napoleon was murdered by poisoning now regard Montholon — despite his assumed devotion to Napoleon — as the most likely suspect.

    Balmain's harsh judgment of Montholon seems to be accurate. His statements, oral and written (e.g., *Récits de la captivite* . . .), are utterly unreliable.

17. Gaspard Gourgaud, (1783–1852). Gaspard, Baron Gourgaud, was born at Versailles; his father was a musician of the royal chapel. At school he showed talent in mathematical studies and later joined the artillery. In 1802 he became junior lieutenant, and thereafter served with credit in the campaigns of 1803–1805, being wounded at Austerlitz. He was present at the siege of Saragossa in 1808, returned to service in Central Europe. In 1811 he became one of the ordnance officers attached to Napoleon, whom he followed closely through the Russian campaign of 1812; he was one of the first to enter the Kremlin. For his services in this campaign he received the title of baron, and became first ordnance officer. In the campaign of 1813 in Saxony he again showed courage and prowess, especially at Leipzig and Hanau; but it was in the first battle of 1814, near to

Brienne, that he rendered the most signal service by killing the leader of a small band of Cossacks who were riding furiously towards Napoleon's tent.

Wounded at the Battle of Montmirail, he recovered in time to be involved in several of the conflicts which followed, distinguishing himself especially at Laon and Reims. Though enrolled among the royal guards of King Louis XVIII of France in the summer of 1814, he embraced the cause of Napoleon during the Hundred Days, was named general and aide-de-camp by Napoleon, and fought at Waterloo.

After the second abdication of the emperor in June 1815, Gourgaud retired with him to Rochefort. It was to Gourgaud that Napoleon entrusted the letter of appeal to the Prince Regent for asylum in England. Gourgaud set off in HMS *Slaney*, but was not allowed to land in England. Determined to share Napoleon's exile, he sailed with him on HMS *Northumberland* to Saint Helena.

Gourgaud, though not enjoying the favour in which basked the other three principal followers, was the most truthful of them all: perhaps for that very reason. Brutally frank persons are apt to be 'gross'; but Balmain does him less than justice. His uncle was Jean-Henri Gourgaud (1746–1809), French actor under the stage name Dugazon, was born in Marseille, the son of Pierre-Antoine Gourgaud, the director of military hospitals there and also an actor.

18. Emmanuel-Augustin-Dieudonné-Joseph, (1766–1842). He was born into a noble family at the castle of Las Cases in Languedoc and educated at the military schools of Vendôme and Paris. After entering the French Royal Navy he took part in various engagements during 1781–1782. Following the outbreak of the Revolution he emigrated, and he spent some years in Germany and ended up in England.
    In 1801 he published in English the original edition of his famous atlas, but following the Peace of Amiens he returned to Paris and issued the first French edition in 1803-1804, called *Atlas historique, genealogique, chronologique et geographique*. The atlas made Las Cases rich. It came to Napoleon's notice only when, in Las Cases's company, he went into exile on St. Helena.

Not until 1810 did he receive much notice from Napoleon's government, which then made him a chamberlain and created him a count of the empire. After the first abdication of the emperor Las Cases retired to England, but returned to serve Napoleon during the Hundred Days. Following the second abdication he withdrew with Napoleon and a few other trusty followers to Rochefort, and then onwards to St Helena. He brought along his eldest son, 14-year-old Emmanuel, "with an intelligence far above his years," according to one historian. Las Cases spoke English — an important asset to Bonaparte. Usually referred to as "young Las Cases," the boy assisted his father in taking down Napoleon's memoirs which thereafter took form in the famous *Mémorial de Ste Hélène*.

Las Cases left St Helena in 1816, and after a short spell at Cape Town he returned to Europe and lived at first at Brussels and later at Paris where he published the *Mémorial*, and soon gained great wealth from it. In 1840 when the expedition set sail for St Helena to bring back Napoleon's body, he was too ill to go, but young Emmanuel who had shared his captivity was able to go.

19. Henri-Gatien, Comte Bertrand, (1773–1844). Henri-Gatien Bertrand was born at Châteauroux, a member of a well-to-do bourgeois family. At the outbreak of the French Revolution, he had just finished his studies at the Prytanée National Militaire, and he entered the army as a volunteer. During the expedition to Egypt, Napoleon named him colonel (1798), then brigadier-general, and after the Battle of Austerlitz his aide-de-camp. His life was henceforth closely bound up with that of Napoleon, who had the fullest confidence in him, honouring him in 1808 with the title of count and at the end of 1813, with the title of Grand Marshal of the Palace. It was Bertrand who in 1809 directed the building of the bridges by which the French army crossed the Danube at Wagram. In 1811, Bertrand was appointed governor for Illyria and during the German campaign of 1813, he commanded IV Corps which he led in the battles of Grossbeeren, Dennewitz and Leipzig. In 1813, after the Battle of Leipzig, it was due to his initiative that the French army was not totally destroyed. He accompanied Napoleon to Elba in 1814, returned with him in 1815, held a command in the Waterloo campaign, and then, after the defeat, accompanied Napoleon to St Helena. Condemned to death in 1816, he did not return to France until after Napoleon's death, and then Louis XVIII granted him amnesty allowing him to retain his rank. Bertrand was elected deputy in 1830 but defeated in 1834. In 1840 he was chosen to accompany the prince de Joinville to St Helena to retrieve and bring Napoleon's remains to France, in what became known as *le retour des cendres*.

   The Bertrand children provided the most constant enjoyment for Napoleon. General Henri Gatien Bertrand, known in Napoleon's Imperial household as "The Grand Marshal", married Fanny Bertrand in 1808. They arrived with three children and settled in a small villa called Hutt's Gate, a mile away from Longwood. A fourth child, Arthur, was born on St Helena in 1817. The Bertrands, particularly the countess, were hoping to limit their stay on the island to not more than a year because of the education needs of their children: Henri aged three, Hortense aged five, and Napoleon aged seven. They had agreed to follow the Emperor into exile before the final destination had been announced, hoping, as did Napoleon, that the final destination would be England. Nevertheless, the Bertrands, who had also accompanied Napoleon to Elba, would stay with Napoleon to the very end. Fanny gave birth to their fourth child Arthur in 1817, and he became Napoleon's favourite member of the family.

20. Barry Edward O'Meara, (1782–1836). Medical Attendant to Napoleon in St Helena, until 25 July 1818. It is extremely interesting that Balmain should state that O'Meara was Lowe's secret agent given what subsequently occurred, and Balmain must have received this information from Lowe personally.

   O'Meara was a native of Co. Cork, and began his medical career as Assistant Surgeon to the 62nd Regiment. But this position he was compelled to resign, because he had contravened the regulations in force by acting as second in a duel.

He then joined the Navy and became Surgeon to the *Goliath* and the *Bellerophon*. He was in this latter ship when Napoleon came on board, and after Maingaud had refused to accompany the Emperor to St Helena, O'Meara was offered the post. He accepted, and remained in attendance until 25 July 1818, when Lowe caused him to be removed from Longwood. He left St Helena on 2 August 1818, and soon after his arrival in England was dismissed the service. O'Meara published his *Exposition* in 1819, in reply to Theodore Hook's *Facts Illustrative*, and in 1822 the famous *Voice* appeared. Besides these, O'Meara was the author of a series of letters to John Finlaison, the Keeper of the Records at the Admiralty, and these can be found in the 'Lowe Papers.' He wrote to Lord Bathurst in 1821, offering to return to Longwood and render what service he could to Napoleon, but the offer was not accepted. O'Meara qualified as a Member of the Royal College of Surgeons in 1825, and lived at 16 Cambridge Terrace, where he died on 10 June 1836. In his will, which is at Somerset House, he directs that the following sentences shall be placed on his tomb: 'I take this opportunity of declaring that with the exception of some unintentional and trifling errors in the *Voice from St Helena*, the book is a faithful narrative of the treatment inflicted upon that great man Napoleon by Sir Hudson Lowe and his subordinates, and that I have even suppressed some facts which although true might have been considered to be exaggerated and not credited.'

21. Thomas William Poppleton, (1775–1827). Poppleton, was the orderly officer of Longwood, who received the "Emperor's Snuff Box" from Napoleon. Poppleton, born in England in 1775, served with General Daumier's regiment, while stationed in Galway. He married, Margaret, daughter of Nicholas Martin of Ross. Subsequently he transferred to the 53rd Foot Regiment, and served in Egypt, and took part in Baird's famous Desert March to India. Having served in the Peninsular Wars, he was appointed orderly officer at Longwood in St Helena and served in this capacity from 10 December 1815 to 24 July 1817. The 53rd (Shropshire) Regiment, or a battalion thereof, was later sent to St Helena to guard Napoleon, who called the Regiment the "Red Regiment", a reference to the colour of their facings, which also gave rise to the Regiment's nickname, the "Brickdusts". One anecdote relates Napoleon's attempt to escape, but the fact is that Napoleon was merely playing with his captor. Napoleon being an expert cavalry rider, and Captain Poppleton (the Captain on guard) only an infantry officer, and little accustomed to riding manoeuvres, the latter had been left far behind by his companion in one of the airings. Napoleon it seems enjoyed most heartily the triumph of galloping away from his keeper, who could only bear the simple jog-trot of his Rosinante. Napoleon had really exceeded the length of his chain, made some romantic and chivalric leaps in his progress, and had climbed some dreadful steeps. Poppleton is said to have been incensed at his conduct, and made a report to the Admiral. The unlucky evil-doer was not allowed to ride out with the Captain for some time, and he was assured, by a rough message from the Admiral, that if he transgressed in such a way again, the sentinels had orders to

level him to the earth. It seems that despite this, the two men became friends and Napoleon made a gift of his snuff box to Poppleton.

22. Any orderly officer at Longwood would have been the 'pet aversion' of the French, but if Balmain had been writing of Poppleton after a longer acquaintance with him he might have changed his opinion of him. Would Napoleon have given a snuff-box to a boor? Furthermore, he was the only orderly officer who had the honour of dining with Napoleon. Unlike those who succeeded him as orderly officers, Poppleton did not dislike his work at Longwood, for when the Fifty-third Regiment was ordered home he applied for permission to remain, but this was not allowed, and his duty at Longwood terminated on 24 July 1817. When he died, in 1927, he was buried in Ireland, and the inscription on the tombstone mentions that he was 'honoured by the esteem of Napoleon.'

23. Gebhard Leberecht von Blücher, 1749–1819.

24. Whether or not this is justified all depends, of course, on the point of view. Ney did say, on 4 April 1814 at Fontainebleau, that all was over; but that was not necessarily treason to the Emperor. On that day Ney's corps mustered only 2,270 officers and men. After the review of the Guard, Marshals Ney, Lefebvre, and Moncey constituted themselves a delegation to inform the Emperor that in their judgment there was nothing left but abdication. During the interview Marshal Macdonald and General Oudinot, who had just arrived, entered and supported Ney. Napoleon finally declared that notwithstanding the contrary opinion of the marshals, he would attack Paris. 'But the army will not march on Paris,' said Ney. 'The army will obey me,' Napoleon replied. 'Sire,' said Ney sternly, 'the army will obey its generals.' Ney won; and that was 'betrayal:' The Emperor dictated to Caulaincourt an act of abdication in favour of his son.

25. Napoleon's fondness for Betsy Balcombe is one of the most pleasing and best known episodes of the St Helena period. He resided at her father's house the Briars, until his removal to Longwood on 10 December 1815. She paid him many visits at Longwood. After her family's removal to England she made the acquaintance of various members of the Bonaparte family, and Napoleon III gave her a tract of land in Algiers. In 1844, she being then Mrs Abell, she published her recollections, which ran into several editions.

   Balcombe probably owed his appointment as purveyor to Longwood to the friendship between Napoleon and his daughter. The business alliance that ensued soon seemed to Lowe to be more intimate than was necessary, and it became evident to the purveyor that he would be more comfortable away from the island. The family accordingly departed in March, 1818, and soon afterward Lowe received proofs of his suspicion that Balcombe had been acting as an intermediary in the transmission of clandestine correspondence to Europe and in negotiating bills drawn by Napoleon. Lord Bathurst, however, appointed him treasurer of the colony of New South Wales, so that the government could not have taken a very serious view of his conduct.

26. The ambiguity of the treaty of 2 August 1815 was embarrassing enough. Lord Eldon, the Lord Chancellor, wrote to Earl Bathurst in September, 1815: 'It strikes me as remarkable that this treaty does not style Bonaparte *a prisoner of war*, nor do I know whether it considers him *as such*. It means certainly that he should be a prisoner after all war is over.' (Report on the Bathurst Manuscripts, 1923, p. 377.)

27. 'Surely St Helena is preferable to Russia,' said Lord Keith in announcing on the *Bellerophon* the place of detention. 'Russia,' exclaimed Napoleon, taken off his guard; 'God preserve me from it.'—Sloan's *Life of Napoleon*.

28. Bertrand, comte Clausel, (1772–1842) was a marshal of France. Clausel had particularly distinguished himself in the Peninsular campaigns. On the first restoration in 1814 he submitted to the Bourbons, but very reluctantly, and when Napoleon escaped from Elba he hastened to join him. During the Hundred Days he commanded the army which operated between the Pyrenees and the Gironde. After Waterloo he refused to recognize the Bourbon government, for which he was declared a traitor and condemned to death, but managed to escape to America. Permitted to return to France in 1819, he was reinstated, later created a marshal, and commanded in the expedition to Algeria (1830).

29. All medical testimony is distinctly opposed to the notion that St Helena is unhealthy. Balmain's account of the mortality in the Sixty-sixth Regiment was based apparently on statements from Longwood, as Dr Henry, surgeon of that regiment, contradicts it in his autobiography. Seaton calls attention to French testimony regarding its healthfulness. In a report published in 1804, *by order of the First Consul*, St Helena was called a 'terrestrial paradise, where health shone in every countenance.'

    Further French testimony was discovered, in an unpublished letter from Baron Gourgaud to his mother, dated from Longwood, 12 January 1816: 'The climate here is very mild, the air very healthy; the change of seasons is only very slightly felt. It is perpetual spring; in short, dear mother, I am very well physically. . . . We are now quite settled in a pretty country house. . . .

30. 'High peaks protect Plantation House, where the vegetation is magnificent. Longwood alone bears the full brunt of the south-easterly gales. For five years and a half Napoleon lived in a perpetual whirlwind.'—Frémeaux, *With Napoleon at St Helena*. (Memoirs of Dr Stokoe).

    The question has occasionally been asked as to why Napoleon was not given the best house on the island, namely, Plantation House. 'It was one of the conditions on which the East India Company allowed the use of the island to the Government, that all the public buildings were to be at the selection of Cockburn as a residence for the Emperor, the Governor's excepted. Plantation House was the centre of the telegraphs or semaphores of the island:'—Seaton.

31. A toise is a pre-Revolutionary measurement in France of approximately 6.4 feet, 1.95 m.

32. As a matter of fact it was Lord Bathurst who was responsible for the deportation of Piontkowski and three (not four) of the Longwood staff. Persuaded by the Latapie affair that Napoleon spent his time in concocting plans of escape, he conceived that these plots were being 'assisted by the number and character of the persons who are about him' and directed Lowe to remove the Pole and three others, to be chosen by the governor. The captain had already been singled out for discipline, since he was suspected of attempting to suborn one of the officers of the Fifty-third Regiment. Napoleon had no particular regard for Piontkowski, and his fellow-exiles do not seem to have mourned his departure.

33. The supposition was well founded. Las Cases's memoirs were the first of all of the writings of the exiles to be published.

34. The hair was really that of the King of Rome, Napoleon's son. Napoléon François Joseph Charles Bonaparte, (1811–1832). Napoleon II was born at the Tuileries Palace in Paris to Napoleon and his second wife, Marie Louise of Austria. As Napoleon I's eldest legitimate son, he was already constitutionally Prince Imperial and heir-apparent, but the Emperor also gave his son the style "His Majesty the King of Rome". Three years later, the First French Empire, to which he was heir, collapsed. Napoleon abdicated the throne in favour of his toddler son, but the Allied Powers, at the insistence of Emperor Alexander I of Russia, refused to recognise the three-year-old as monarch. In April 1814 Marie Louise retired to Austria with young Napoleon. He died of tuberculosis at Schönbrunn Palace in Vienna in 1832. The Emperor Napoleon never saw his son again after 1814.

35. Philippe Welle, A botanist who came out to St Helena with the Austrian Commissioner, Baron Stürmer, in the *Orontes*. He arrived on 18 June 1816, and was charged by Marchand's mother, who was nurse to the King of Rome, with a letter containing a lock of the King of Rome's hair. This he delivered to Marchand, who transmitted it to Napoleon. The transaction aroused Lowe's suspicions, and Welle left the Island on 1 March 1817.

36. Stürmer, although beyond doubt blameworthy in this affair, was in a position of rather peculiar difficulty. Many believed that he came to St Helena with secret instructions to arrange a reconciliation between Napoleon and his father-in-law. These suspicions were strengthened when it was found that he brought with him an emissary from the imperial gardens at Schönbrunn, on a pretended botanical expedition. That the Emperor Francis had sent a man all the way from Vienna simply to collect plants was not believed. When it was learned that the botanist had been entrusted with a lock of the hair of Napoleon's son, which he had succeeded in passing to Napoleon without the governor's knowledge, an Austrian conspiracy seemed to be proved.

    'It was on account of affairs of this kind,' says Norwood Young, 'that Sir Hudson Lowe, who had in fact been the only upright and honourable man of all concerned, was handed down to future generations as a heartless and cruel jailer. Stürmer was guilty of underhand conduct, and, being found out by Lowe, he turned on that official and abused him in reports which have obtained a certain amount of credence. The result is that while every person concerned was worthy of censure except Lowe, he alone has had to carry the stigma of disgrace.'

The conduct of Stürmer naturally affected the prestige of the commissioners as a body, and was one of the chief reasons given later for his recall.

37. A villain in European folk tales who marries several wives and murders them in turn.

38. Quoted by Balmain in English.

39. Previously to coming to table, the guest makes a profound inclination of the body, or actual prostration, according to the rank of the host. [Note accompanying the translation.]

40. Excellently, perhaps, but with a terrible diffuseness. Seaton says he was not a good letter-writer. His sentences are long and involved, as inspection of such of them as are quoted in this volume will show. Where there is a difference of opinion, correspondence only aggravates a dispute instead of allaying it, unless there is very good will on both sides. Napoleon's determination to hold no personal intercourse with the governor necessitated a voluminous correspondence, which in itself would have been formidable enough, but which created additional trouble when couched in the rhetorical and diplomatic style affected by the exiles. The French were delighted to have the opportunity of this correspondence. It gave them something to do, and something in which the chances were they could come off best. To all who would look they showed their letters and the governor's replies with great gusto, while Lowe kept his correspondence secret and brooded over it.

41. Rear-Admiral Robert Plampin, (1762–1834). Plampin had lived for some time in France and had thus acquired proficiency in the language; in 1793 he served in Toulon as aide-de-camp to Lord Hood, until the end of the siege of that town. He saw much service in the Far East, and was in the Mediterranean for some years toward the end of the war. He was Commander-in-Chief of the St Helena and Cape of Good Hope Naval Stations from July 1817, to July 1820. Plampin arrived in HMS *Conqueror* on 29 June 1817. He lived at the Briars after the Balcombe family left. While in command of the St Helena Station, Plampin played a noteworthy part in the arrangements made for the safe custody of Napoleon, and throughout he was a firm supporter of the policy of Sir Hudson Lowe. He was especially singled out as the subject of the Revd Mr Boys' strictures from the pulpit. The reason for this attitude on the part of Mr Boys is evident from the following extract from the autobiographical manuscript of Dr Stokoe, the Surgeon of the *Conqueror: On the Admiral's first visit to Plantation House he was not accompanied by his Lady. This excited the surprise of Lady Lowe, and inquiry was immediately set on foot amongst the officers of the Flag-ship to ascertain if the Admiral was a married man. No satisfactory information being obtained on that head, it was reported that the Admiral would soon be recalled*

and his Lady immediately sent off the Island. He was even preached at from the pulpit. However, he soon found means to make his peace with the Governor, and the preaching was discontinued 'by order.' Plampin showed no sympathy with the lot of Bonaparte, and always spoke of him in the most disparaging terms. His attitude towards Mr Stokoe, the Surgeon of the *Conqueror*, who attended Napoleon for three days in 1819, was unduly harsh, and it was largely owing to the Admiral's attitude at the court martial that Stokoe was dismissed the Navy. Plampin had two interviews with the Emperor, on 3 July and 5 September 1817. The conversation turned upon the amount of water carried on board ship, and the experiences of the Admiral when cruising off Toulon. The opinion of Napoleon concerning Plampin was no more favourable than the Admiral's concerning him.

42. Colonel Muiron had been killed at Napoleon's side in the battle of Arcola.

43. This was a present from the Hon. John Elphinstone, and was of a somewhat different character from similar gifts sent from time to time by members of the Opposition in that it was partly a mark of gratitude to the Emperor for having saved the life of the donor's brother, who had been severely wounded and made a prisoner on the day before Waterloo. In sending the chessmen, marked with eagles, N., and a crown, Elphinstone's purpose, of course, was to draw attention to the title without actually transgressing the rule against mentioning it. Lowe's letter to Bertrand, mentioned by Balmain, said that if he were to act in strict conformity with the established rules he ought to delay sending the pieces, but that, as he had promised that the boxes should follow the letter, he had no alternative but to forward them. The good-will of Lowe is evident enough in this letter, but the last sentence is expressed with that ungraciousness which often justified the title of boor. 'Sir Hudson Lowe is a very good man with very disagreeable manners, or, to put it better, knowing very little of those of society; but loyal and full of honour. As Governor he is an unbearable man, who displeases and must displease everyone.' So wrote, at about this time, Montchenu in a letter to the Marquis d'Osmond, French ambassador at London, as quoted in the *Report on the Bathurst Manuscripts* (London, 1923).

44. *Les officiers de santé vous diront qu'il n'y a plus de tems à perdre, que dans 3 ou 4 semaines peut-être, il ne sera plus tems.*

45. Prominent Whigs such as Elphinstone, Holland, Sir Robert Wilson, the Duke of Bedford, and J. C. Hobhouse.

46. Denzil Ibbetson, (1788–1857), entered the commissariat department of the army as clerk in 1808, and went through the Peninsular Campaign. In 1814 he was promoted assistant commissary-general and was ordered to St Helena in 1815. He sailed on board the *Northumberland* with Napoleon and remained on the island until 1823. He thus has the distinction of being one of the four British officers who remained in St Helena during the whole period of the captivity. For the first three years of his stay Ibbetson had little to do with Longwood, for the purveyorship was in the hands of Balcombe, Fowler & Company; but after the

departure of Balcombe, Ibbetson assumed charge, and apparently performed his duties to Lowe's satisfaction, for the latter wrote a highly eulogistic letter afterward. He was an amateur artist of no small skill, and both on board ship and on the island made many sketches of Napoleon and his followers. For a fuller account of one of the most interesting of the British officers during the captivity, see the article by A. M. Broadley in the *Century Magazine*: April, 1912.

47. Dr Alexander Baxter, (1777–1841), had first come into contact with Lowe when he was appointed surgeon to the Royal Corsican Rangers in 1805, and was present with him at the surrender of Capri in 1808. He saw considerable active service extending from 1799 to 1814. In the latter year he served with the troops in America and was present at the battle of Bladensburg. At the request of Lowe he was next appointed deputy inspector of hospitals in St Helena and arrived with the Governor in April, 1816. He remained on the island until 1819, and during all that time, especially after O'Meara's removal from Longwood, played a most important part in the difficult situations which arose regarding medical attendance on the Emperor.

48. The 1924 publication in New York of a new translation of this manuscript has again attracted attention to an implied attempt to fasten its authorship on Napoleon. The Emperor himself first saw the published book (originally published simultaneously in French and English by Murray in April, 1817) when it was shown him by Montholon in September of that year, and his only connection with it seems to have been the forty-four criticisms which he thereupon wrote. After several of the St Helena exiles had been taxed with the authorship, other and greater writers, e. g., Constant, Mme. de Staël, were accused; but it is now generally agreed that the author was Lullin de Chateauvieux (1772–1841), and the copy in the Library of Congress is attributed to this little known Swiss philosopher. 'A keen observer and a fine mind, he followed closely the intricate political movements of the time, into which his manifold relations with the leaders who played the principal rôles permitted him to gain a wonderful insight. He was therefore well equipped for venturing the *tour de force* of writing the exile's professed own apology of his life, the exposition of his projects and views, and above all to give expression to his contempt for the human species. But . . . it was not long before numerous anachronisms and opinions which could not possibly have belonged to the Emperor were being demonstrated by competent critics.'—Charles Martel, in the *American Historical Review*, January, 1925. Napoleon specifically disavowed the manuscript in his will.

49. However, see report No. 10 of 1816 (p. 65).

50. It did not seem necessary to remember that she had been under no compulsion in the first place to go to St Helena.

51. Princess Charlotte, only child of the Prince of Wales (the Prince Regent, later George IV) and his wife, Caroline of Brunswick, was of a temperament which might well have sympathized with Napoleon's misfortunes. By nature impulsive,

capricious, and vehement, she herself had always longed for liberty, but had possessed it only during the one year of her marriage. In May, 1816, the princess married Prince Leopold of Saxe-Coburg (later King Leopold I of Belgium) and died on November 6, 1817.

52. General Labédoyère greatly distinguished himself at Waterloo and after the battle was reckless in his championship of the cause of Napoleon II. The Duchesse d'Angoulême took the initiative, and he was court-martialled and shot on 19 August 1815. Ney's trial was even more of a hollow sham. He was shot on 7 December 1815.

53. From the beginning of Act V, Scene l, of Corneille's *Cinna*.

54. John Stokoe, (1775–1852), surgeon to the *Conqueror*, was summoned to attend Napoleon on 17 January 1819 (his first visit), and between that day and 21 January he paid the emperor five visits. But in doing so, as Balmain's reports will show, he had incurred Lowe's displeasure. It is difficult to understand why Stokoe was treated so harshly in the court-martial unless partisanship on the judges' part is assumed. Paul Frémeaux has built a book around Stokoe: *Napoleon Prisonnier*; Paris, 1902, in which he details the generosity of various members of the Bonaparte family to Stokoe after his dismissal from the navy. Madame Mère, Cardinal Fesch, Louis, and Joseph all showed their gratitude in very practical forms.

55. Lieutenant-Colonel Lyster had replaced Captain Blakeney as orderly officer at Longwood. 'He is an Irishman;' Balmain had written on 15 July, 'rather elderly, and very honest. In 1793 he was a major at Ajaccio, where he knew the Bonaparte family. Napoleon detests him and already has his door refused to him:'

56. James R. Verling (1787–1858) served throughout the Peninsular Campaign. In 1815 he was ordered to St Helena in medical charge of the artillery troops destined for that island, and sailed in the *Northumberland* with Napoleon. As Balmain reports, Verling was appointed to reside at Longwood after the removal of O'Meara, but when Napoleon refused to see any doctor appointed by Lowe, Verling found himself without occupation. He continued in residence until he was relieved by the arrival of Antommarchi (20 September 1819). He left the island in April, 1820, and was almost unique in carrying away with him the regard of both the governor and the French exiles. He subsequently rose to high rank in the army. While at Longwood he compiled a most interesting journal, which is now in the *Archives Nationales* in Paris.

57. After Napoleon's death and Lowe's return to England, the latter became almost an outcast socially and politically. In 1825 he was made commander of the troops in Ceylon, a post quite beneath his rank and experience. He came back to England in 1831, but the Whigs were in power, and he obtained no further employment. When he was insulted in the House of Lords, Wellington came to his defence most generously, but would do nothing more practical for him. When almost too late, the government attempted to repair its injustices, and in 1842 he was made a G.C.M.G. and appointed colonel of the Fiftieth Regiment. Two years later he

died, almost in poverty. 'Lowe was not the only distinguished public servant who, on returning from arduous duty on a distant station, has become the victim of party politicians. But even in that long-suffering class his fate was exceptional.'– N. Young.

58. John VI of Portugal. Expelled when General Junot entered Lisbon in 1806, the royal family took refuge in Brazil, and the two countries in 1815 were given the title of the United Kingdom of Portugal, Brazil, and Algarves. The union was dissolved, however, when John returned to Portugal in 1822 and his son Pedro was proclaimed emperor of Brazil.

59. Matthew Livingstone, superintendent of the East India Company's medical establishment in St Helena, was frequently called to attend the Bertrands and the Montholons. He attended the post-mortem examination of Napoleon, and when asked by Lowe whether he observed anything abnormal in the liver, he replied in the negative.

60. Ricketts was a cousin of the prime minister. The account which he gave of the interview confirms Balmain's impression that it was a masquerade. On this, however, as on other occasions, the good manners of a visitor raised hopes at Longwood which were doomed to disappointment. In a despatch to Lowe Lord Bathurst wrote: 'Nothing could have been more fortunate than Mr Ricketts's visit. He has given the most satisfactory reports concerning the real state of the business, and saw through all the manoeuvres which were practised to impose upon him.'

61. O'Meara's name, however, was struck off the list of naval surgeons early in the year 1819, without pension.

62. When a surgeon was precisely what was needed. Neither O'Meara nor Antommarchi entertained the slightest suspicion that Napoleon was suffering from cancer. At the post-mortem 'no unhealthy appearance was observed in the liver.' At that time, of course, very little was known of cancer of the stomach.

63. The Ile de France was Mauritius. The Portuguese discovered the island in 1507, the Dutch settled on the island in 1638 and abandoned it in 1710. Five years later, the island became a French colony and was renamed Ile de France. The British took control of Mauritius in 1810. It became independent in 1968.

64. Archibald Arnott came to St Helena with his regiment in 1819, and on 21 April 1821 paid his first professional visit to Napoleon. He quickly established excellent relations and continued in constant attendance until the end. He attended the post-mortem and in 1822 published *An Account of the Last Illness of Napoleon*.

65. An original copy of this report was inserted in Balmain's manuscript.

66. The Lowe Papers mention a conversation with Balmain on the subject of the bullocks. Balmain remarked that he thought it a cruel kind of diversion to kill animals in this way, but that would not be the Corsican feeling. Pope Pius IX, another Italian prisoner, amused himself by shooting sparrows. Napoleon kept a carbine in his study at Malmaison and used to fire from inside the room at any birds which might come within range, including even some of Josephine's pets.